Dear Goldie Hawn,
Dear Leonard Cohen

Claudia Sternbach

Published by Unruly Voices
unrulyvoices.com

An imprint of Paper Angel Press
paperangelpress.com

ISBN 978-1-953469-98-4 (Hardcover)

10 9 8 7 6 5 4 3 2 1

FIRST EDITION

For Michael

Contents

Dear Goldie Hawn, Dear Leonard Cohen

Dear Johannes Vermeer,

I had no idea you would be waiting for me that day. I was about to have my first appointment with a psychiatrist where I would, I assumed, be expected to spill my guts, and I was terrified.

I wonder, if I had known that, along with the doctor, your "Girl with a Pearl Earring" was waiting for me on the other side of the door, would I have been less nervous? It is, after all, my favorite of yours. My sisters loved it as well.

I recall clearly that initial appointment. Details are still crisp and sharp. Like an early fall day, which it was.

The waiting room was more hallway than actual room. I was the only person in the space and the door to the office was shut. This was my first visit to a psychiatrist, so I was unsure of the protocol. Do I knock? Do I wait for someone to come and fetch me?

Nervous about this appointment, I forgot to arm myself with reading material. I was in the middle of a compelling novel and desperately wished I had tucked it into my bag. I contemplated leaving. Just slipping back out the door and driving back home. I would have sent the good doctor a check to cover the wasted hour. I swear.

There was a stairwell opposite me, and a young, professional looking woman was climbing the stairs. Her sleek blonde hair, pulled back into a smooth top knot, came into view first. She was clutching half a dozen or so manila folders against her chest. She smiled as she saw me. I knew her. She went to school with my daughter. Her mother is a great friend of mine. She paused and I stood up and embraced her. She glanced at the closed door and then back at me. Then went on her way down the hall to her own office. She is an attorney in this building.

Now escape was no longer an option. She had seen me.

I wondered if she was curious about why I was there. I felt horribly self-conscious. But then I realized that she must know. Everyone knows. I have lost my sister, and in losing her, I have also lost most of my family. Coping has become almost unbearable. My husband, Michael, has forced my hand. He has insisted I need to get help. Professional help. So there I was, waiting for that help. That miracle, to open the door and invite me in.

Three pages into a People magazine, the doctor stepped out of his office and approached me. He held out his hand and smiled. He had such a kind face and his voice was gentle as he introduced himself and gestured for me to follow.

In his office was a print of "Girl with a Pearl Earring". I stood, transfixed. My eyes filled as I recalled introducing both of my sisters to you, Johannes Vermeer. To this painting in particular.

I avoided looking at the doctor as I took a seat, instead focusing on The Girl.

He had placed a large box of tissues next to one chair, so it was obvious I was meant to sit there. He lowered himself into the chair opposite and reached over, pulled a Kleenex from the box and handed it to me.

Then we sat quietly. There was a large window, and I watched as the coastal fog swirled outside, temporarily hiding the eucalyptus trees from view. It felt as if there were three of us in the room. The doctor, me, and The Girl watching over us. And with her there, in that room, I knew I was exactly where I was supposed to be.

Once composed, I smiled. I apologized for my emotional break.

He simply shook his head and told me there was no need.

I assumed that it was not uncommon for someone to fall apart in his office. I wondered if he bought his boxes of tissue at Costco.

"Tell me," he asked. "Why have you come?"

Because I am broken. Because I no longer understand what love is. Because I don't know where I belong. Or if I ever belonged. Because I am sitting at the bottom of the pool and do not want to come to the surface.

But I did not say these things.

"Because my husband is afraid to leave me alone," I told him. "He is exhausted by my sadness. And I am afraid that if I can't get better, be better, he will leave. And I would not blame him. If I could leave me, I would. And that too scares the shit out of him. And me."

Just saying the words out loud settled me. My eyes were dry. My breathing steady. I had spoken the truth and the sky did not fall. Fuck Chicken Little.

Maybe I can do this. Maybe I can. "My sister died," I said.

"Is this the first loss you have experienced?" he asked. "Not at all," I replied, "Not by a long shot".

"Have you any ideas about why this particular loss is so difficult?" "Yes," I said, and then felt my throat begin to constrict.

Once again, the room was silent as I tried to compose myself. If I opened my mouth, I was afraid the words would spill out like a waterfall after a heavy storm and drown us both. And what if, after telling my story, he agreed that I have little or no value. That I am, in fact, unloveable?

I watched him carefully, trying to read his expression. I watched the small clock, which rested on the table between us. I did not want to overstay my welcome. I was afraid of taking up too much of his time. As if reading my mind, he told me we were in no rush.

I believed him, but did I trust him?

I had nothing to lose. So, I began. I described one of the last times I was with my younger sisters, Carol and Cheryl and Carol's wife. Carol, lying in bed dying, her twin, Cheryl sitting next to me. Carol's wife, standing as if on stage, in front of us.

I began to recount the evening. I have replayed it in my mind a thousand times, so I did not hesitate in the telling. I live it over and over again every night. I close my eyes and I am there, in that room.

I did not look at his face as I spoke. As I described what took place I focused on The Girl.

I had just given Carol a small spoonful of lemon sorbet, I explained. The cool, tart treat one of the only foods left that she enjoyed.

I began with Carol's wife's opening statement. "Claude, look at me," she said.

"I have never liked you," she continued. "Never. You should know that," she added. "Especially now. It is time you knew."

"This," she said, indicating herself, "is a façade," she stated with a smile. "You have never known me. Cheryl does."

She then went on to explain just how much she detested me. How, when I cared for my sister, both this time and the first time she had cancer, she couldn't stand coming home and the end of the day knowing I was there.

"Oh," she added, "I did appreciate that you cooked dinner each night. I especially liked the avocado and mango salad."

(One ripe avocado, one ripe mango. Slice each and fan out on a salad plate. Squeeze lime over it all and sprinkle with salt. Delicious!)

I was having a difficult time understanding her words. Like hearing a foreign language for the first time. But the expression on her face said it all. There was hate in her eyes. And she was so cool, calm. As if she had rehearsed this a thousand times. As if she had been waiting for the perfect moment. And this, she decided, was it?

Then, as if fearful that I had not understood her completely, she stated again how much she disliked me and always has.

"And," she declared, "Cheryl is my soulmate."

Fuck, I detest that lame-ass phrase.

And wait, she was married to Carol, who would be gone in a matter of days. But she was claiming Cheryl as hers now?

I was at a loss.

Carol closed her eyes and tears ran down her cheeks. Cheryl stared at the floor while I sat, stunned. The lecture went on for what seemed like hours.

I thought about all of the weekends I spent cooking organic food, blending it into a baby food constancy, and filling small, single portion containers to take with me to my sister's house so she might have healthy food to eat after her first bout of cancer. How I spent weeks and weeks driving back and forth, spending two and three nights at a time helping to care for her.

I asked if that had no value. I was met with silence.

I reminded them all that a few years earlier when I had breast cancer, none of them even came to visit, let alone bring me food or offer to help. And I never was angry. As the eldest of the three of us, that was the pattern I set. I could take care of myself.

"Well, we probably should have," said Cheryl, looking down at the floor. The discussion was over.

Cheryl and I shared a bed that night. She lay still and never uttered a word of comfort. I assumed she was sleeping. I was not. I wanted to leave the house and drive home to Michael. But two things stopped me. I had no idea how to disarm the alarm which I knew was set, and I still wanted time with Carol.

But I had never felt so unwanted, ever. Anywhere.

In the morning, after getting no sleep at all, after vomiting in the guest bathroom and wanting nothing more than to curl up on the floor, I went out to my car to begin the long drive home. I was clearly not wanted there. Carol's wife had made that perfectly clear. Cheryl walked out with me.

Why, I wanted to know, had that happened? "And why didn't you defend me?" I asked her.

"Because I agreed with her," said my sister. "But what did I do?" I asked.

"You are just different," she replied and shrugged her shoulders. I am different. Which apparently makes me unloveable.

This, I explained to the doctor, was my story. This was why my sister's death has been almost impossible to bear. This was why I was sitting there in his office, because in the days after that evening, my phone calls to my sister were refused. Because after her death, there were ceremonies where her ashes were scattered, but I was never informed.

Because cancer took one of my sisters and circumstances took the other. Because Cheryl chose Her and I had had no idea we were in a competition. And in doing so I lost Cheryl and her children and grandchildren in one fell swoop. My family.

Strangely, my tears had stopped and I was almost composed. The doctor seemed pleased that I had said this much, but disturbed at the tale.

I stared at The Girl while waiting for his response.

Do you know, Mr. Vermeer, what a soothing presence she has?

The doctor leaned towards me, but did not breech the professional space between doctor and patient. He placed his hand on his chest, over his heart.

"Cruelty is difficult to understand," he said, "And some people are very cruel." A simple explanation.

And then our time was up.

But not our relationship. Each week I drove to his office, sat in the hall and waited for him to invite me in. Some days I felt as if progress was made; other days I left his office and sat in my car feeling raw and exposed, as though any protective outer shell I may have had had been peeled away and I was left more vulnerable than a new born. Then one day, weeks into this adventure, he gave me some homework.

We had both of us pretty much come to understand the reality of the situation and he, unbeknownst to me, was on a tight time schedule. We had work to do. And we did not have all the time in the world after all. Cancer had come into his life as well. He would not be victorious.

"Next week, tell me about the people who have added to your life," he said. "Tell me who they are and let's see how we might proceed. Might tip the scales in your favor. Yes, you have lost people who you dearly loved. But let's look at what is left."

Who, he wanted to know, had added to my life. Not just the obvious choices, he said, but those who have helped shape me, guide me in unexpected ways.

"What would you say to them if you could?" he asked. "What would you say to Carol?"

That night I began to list their names. And I began to write. To people I knew, to total Strangers, and to my late sister. Perhaps in doing this I might find answers. Perhaps not. I began with Goldie Hawn, as she figured into my first taste of being really free. Independent. I began to measure myself against her, that smiling girl who seemed to laugh at everything, no matter the circumstances. It is something I have always tried to do. Lately though, I had difficulty even smiling.

At his memorial service I was able to tell his daughter how much he meant to me. She embraced me, something he never did, being the consummate professional. She told me how much it meant to hear that about her father. I wish I had had the chance to tell him. He threw me a life line. He helped pull me up from the bottom of the pool.

All under the watchful gaze of your most famous work of art, "Girl with a Pearl Earring".

Yours,
Claudia

Johannes Vermeer, a Dutch painter, was born in 1632. I did not know him. Famous for his paintings of the lives of the middle-class and his use of light, he saw his greatest success after his death. Which actually means he didn't ever see it after all. At the time of his death, his wife and children were found to be penniless. In debt, in fact.

A few years ago, one of his paintings brought in 40 million dollars at auction. Oh, to have grabbed up a couple when he was just a beginner!

And so it began ...

Dear Goldie Hawn,

This letter is long overdue. I've put things off. I have, on occasion, neglected to follow through on a jury summons.

Christmas cards, when sent at all, have become April Fools cards. I can't tell you when I last went to the dentist.

Lately, however, I have felt the need to catch up on things of importance, which brings me to you.

Have you ever been lucky enough to fly across the Atlantic in a passenger-free 747? Been able to slip out of your day clothes, for me an orange and brown uniform made entirely out of polyester with an inability to wrinkle, but hung up in the closet anyway and replaced with a brown trench coat, which doubled as a bathrobe for curling up on a full row of passenger-free seats to nap as the flight deck crew navigated us across the sea? If not, you have missed something quite marvelous.

In the early 1970s I was a flight attendant with World Airways. Life on the ground had become too complicated for me, so my options were to take up deep sea diving and spend my days surrounded by kelp forests and ocean creatures or take to the sky.

I chose the clouds. I wanted to see what was above them. To burst through and explore the heavens. Plus, I had never been anywhere and felt it was about time.

I was either trying to find myself or lose myself. I confess I still don't know which.

My first flight was to Malaga, Spain. Before that I had been on a plane exactly one time. I had flown from San Francisco to Los Angeles. Now, here I was on a fully-loaded 747, three hundred passengers if I recall correctly, all of whom assumed I had some kind of airline experience. Standing in the center aisle presenting the safety instructions, explaining that the seat cushions doubled as flotation devices should we have to "ditch"the aircraft in the deep blue sea, I tried not to imagine how cold the water would be and how flimsy our promised salvation. Confidence, I hoped, was on my face. Yes, you may count on me, was the image I hoped I was projecting.

Minutes later, buckled into my own crew jump-seat, I listened to the roar of the engines as we prepared to take off. I thrilled to the power and force and as we lifted, I felt my stomach drop, my armpits became damp, my hands shook enough for me to notice, but no one else. We were on our way. And we had, in our care, hundreds of passengers, all of whom sold mattresses.

We were a charter company, so it was not unusual to have a group of travelers who all did the same thing.

Once, Goldie, we took hundreds of nuns to Rome. It was like taking a group of teenage girls to meet the Beatles.

But that is another story.

Many of the flights were "all inclusive". Where just weeks earlier I had taken great pride in how many cocktails I could distribute in an evening at the country western bar where I worked five nights a week, I now felt I had made a great leap in my professional career. I was pouring drinks in the sky!

The mattress folks drank the plane dry somewhere over the mid-Atlantic. Thankfully we had you along to keep the grumbling to a minimum. We had your film, "Butterflies are Free", as the in-flight entertainment.

Goldie, remember before there were screens at every seat and instead a large screen dropped down at the front of each cabin and a film was shown to help pass the time? First, we would announce the movie, then ask that passengers pull down the shades at their windows for optimal viewing, and then there you were up on the screen keeping everyone occupied while we hurried up and down the aisles scooping up trash, handing out blankets and pillows, refilling drinks and in the galleys, stomping garbage down into the bins so they could be safely secured.

I was so frustrated. I wanted to sit and watch the film. I wanted to know what was going on with the cute blind guy.

I will confess something quite embarrassing right now. There were people, my own mother among them, who claimed to notice a resemblance between us. You look like her, my mother said when she would see you on "Laugh-In". You sound like her, she would add.

Passengers said the same thing as I hurried through the darkened cabin.

I was quite flattered. Who wouldn't be? But, as I had one foot, ankle-deep, stomping down rejected meals while hanging onto the metal bin for balance, I knew for a fact I wasn't you. But it didn't matter. With my new uniform, wings pinned to my chest, no apartment to go home to, no car needing payments, no "love interest" awaiting my return, I was no longer the girl I had been. I was as free as, well, a butterfly.

After dropping off our tired, hungover mattress sellers in Malaga, we needed to get the plane to Boston in order to pick up another charter. The flight deck crew bid us farewell and a fresh flight deck crew came on board. As flight attendants, our only job was to rotate caring for them. Meals, coffee, meals again. And, we were allowed to run the film.

The lining of our raincoats was smooth to the touch. The pillows and blankets were plentiful. We determined who would be on duty when, wrote up the schedule, and then made ourselves comfortable in our cozy nests above the clouds.

Oh, dear Goldie. I loved the movie. I imagined being you, or at least the character you played in the film. I understood her wish to be loved. And to love. She was brave and funny and had such an open heart.

We ran "Butterflies are Free" for an entire month. You were my companion as I traveled to places I had never been before. You were with me on the long, tiring flights back home. To Europeans you became the face of young American women. A gentleman from Frankfurt once asked me if all of the girls in the United States were as free as you were in that movie.

I told him no. But some of us were working on it.

Yours, with gratitude,
Claudia

Goldie Hawn, middle name Jeanne, was born in 1945. She does not look her age! Early in her career, from 1968-1970, she appeared in the sketch comedy television show Rowan & Martin's Laugh-In *where her wide smile and infectious giggle brightened up living rooms all around the country. She spent quite a lot of time in a bikini, go-go dancing in a cage.*

YouTube it!

In 1972, she made the film Butterflies are Free, *based on a play written by Leonard Gershe. Edward Albert was the blind love interest. She went on to have a terrific career in films, but* Butterflies are Free *is my favorite.*

Rent it!

Dear Leonard Cohen,

Your voice fills my car as I drive through the Santa
Cruz Mountains in Northern California on my way to
visit my mother in her assisted living facility. I turn up
the volume and can almost feel your breath in my ear.
You are that close. When you sing, whisper, pray, your
voice reaches the marrow in my bones. I carry your
words with me as I sit with her at lunch, her table mates
all in their wheelchairs, some with hair so white it
startles, some wearing wigs, some with their smooth,
bare skulls looking more like infants than fully grown
adults, nodding over their noon day meal.

I am glad you left this world before ending up
here, or someplace like this.

Oh, it isn't as if this is a bad place. The staff is
kind, not a holiday goes by that they don't decorate like
gang busters. The food is decent. My mother has times
where she is content. You notice I don't say "happy".
She is fully aware of her living situation. Most of the
residents are. They are at the last station, waiting. One

by one they depart. The sirens silent as they are taken away.

I have one sister. She and I have tried to share the responsibility. But I confess, she has done more. She is closer in distance. My mother, I believe, understands.

I once had two sisters. Lost one to cancer a few years ago. I miss her. I curse the cancer. So, I listen to you. You whisper in my ear. Your breath is hot. I can feel your whiskers against my cheek.

The surviving sister, I have lost her too. A rip in the family fabric which seems impossible to mend. So, I fill the car with your voice and I listen, listen. You keep me company as I descend into my own darkness. When you sing of being tired and angry all the time, I am your companion just as you are mine.

I read someplace that there are actually 82 verses to "Hallelujah", but that you have never recorded them all. I wish you had. I believe I would choose to listen to that prayer every day.

We grew old together, Leonard. Out in my garage, along with my daughter's tricycle and my grandson's old stroller, are albums you recorded decades ago. Your hair dark and shaggy. Mine was long and blonde. Your voice had not yet reached the depths it would in years to come. The older you got, the more you spoke, sang, for me. To me. I spend hours trying to understand the words. The religiosity of your lyrics.

I believe in nothing heavenly. No Father, Son, or Holy Ghost. If there is something or someone waiting, "out there", I hope it is you. It is you, Leonard, that I can imagine existing on some other plane. Sitting with your guitar and with a gravelly whisper, making me feel less alone.

Heading back home after visiting my mother I listen to "You Want it Darker" and feel every word is being spoken on my behalf. I listen to "Leaving the Table" and weep as I drive up and over the mountain, through the redwoods, back to the foggy coast and home.

Thank you for that. For finding a way to keep me company as I head towards the dark. I am not alone. I have you.

I wish you knew. Perhaps you do?

Claudia

Leonard Cohen was born in Canada in 1934. He sadly died in 2016. He was a poet, singer songwriter, and novelist. I imagine he was a magnet to women on both sides of our northern border. I totally would have slept with him! (Of course I mean before Michael!)

I do adore a tortured soul.

He won several awards over his long career, including being inducted into the Rock and Roll Hall of Fame and the Glenn Gould Prize.

Dear Hayley Mills,

Well, I don't suppose you ever expected to hear from me! I was never one of those little girls who wrote fan letters to their favorite movie stars. If I had been, you would have received one. But nope, I was much too busy doing the important things that 10-year-olds just have to do.

Spying on my little sisters. Sneaking my mother's razor to attempt my first leg-shave. Listening in on the telephone party line. Reading my mother's movie magazines.

Sneaking into her closet and trying on her pink leather high heels. Who could possibly find the time for a proper thank-you letter? So why now?

Bear with me, please, Hayley.

My daughter is an actor. A few years ago, she was cast in a play in London. My husband, Michael, and I flew, as they say, across the pond, to see it. It has been a while, but I doubt I shall ever forget what it felt like to watch her on that stage. She seemed to own it. There wasn't a moment of hesitation in her performance.

This was my baby girl? Fearless.

Her director was the brilliant Michael Attenborough. The assistant to the director was your son.

After the performance we gathered in the cafe area of the theater. I chose to sit at the end of a small bar, sipping champagne. Your son, your delightful, highly complementary son, sat down on the stool next to me. I introduced myself, "the actress's mother," and he, in turn, introduced himself.

He looks like you, Hayley. As we sat there, I became a 10-year-old once again, although I doubt he noticed it.

How could this be? How had the world turned so many times with both you and I going in so many directions for decades and yet, as if by some incredible master plan, our children ended up working on a play together and I ended up on a barstool next to your son while waiting for my daughter to come from backstage?

Serendipity?

Who can say? But as we sat, I thought about how much joy you had brought to me when I was a young girl. I adored all of your films. But without a doubt, "The Parent Trap" was the one I returned to again and again. That was the movie that spoke to me the most. It motivated me!

There were many reasons.

My parents were divorced!

I had twin sisters!

I went to summer camp!

I believed I could trick my parents into getting married again!

There were a few glitches in every plan I hatched, however. First, I didn't have a twin; I was simply twin-adjacent. And they had no interest in my finagling and scheming.

Second, my father had remarried and had an entirely new family with which he was apparently very happy. Attached even. And really, that fact rendered any of the possible solutions to "my" problem pointless.

Plus, I'm not sure that my mother would have welcomed him with open arms and tuna casserole. He had married one of her best friends and adopted one of her children.

If that isn't rude, I don't know what is!

Back to the drawing board. Or to be more precise, back to the movies to see if I might glean some small hint as to how I might correct this wrong!

I suppose the timing was off. Perhaps if the movie had been made a few years earlier, I could have tried out some of your clever pranks and convinced my father that it was my mother he loved, not this other woman with two girls. Maybe then I would be writing to say "thank you" for showing me how to get my dad to come back home.

But that isn't your fault, Hayley. Nope. You were given the script when you were given the script. Perhaps it was perfectly timed for some other little girl. Perhaps her father returned home and never left again. It could be, don't you think?

So here I am in my seventh decade and finally writing to thank you for making that movie. For giving me hope and showing me how to be spunky and brave, with or without a father, no matter what.

I wish I could have shared all of this with your son. But being a mother of a young woman whom I knew would be mortified if, the next day, at the theater he had said to her, "Man, some wacky mom you have!" I only asked him to give you my best.

But then again, he was such a dear gentleman, raised so well, he might have only smiled as she came through the doors and kept silent.

With admiration and fond memories,
Claudia

Hayley Mills is an English actress, born in 1946. She comes from quite an acting family. She is the daughter of Sir John Mills and the sister of actress Juliet Mills. Not only was she the star of The Parent Trap *in 1961, but she also played the part of Pollyanna in the film of the same name.*

I disliked that movie, but do not hold that against her. She is still acting! Often on stage!

And she raised a very cordial young man.

Dear Bill Cosby,

Well, you are not all you were cracked up to be. What a nasty surprise it has been to find out that you are far from being "America's Dad". And before I go any further, let me say I believe each and every woman who has accused you of gross and disgusting sexual behavior. I have thought long and hard about writing to you.

Why am I corresponding with you?

Well, because one summer night in a casino in Nevada, I sat with my mother and a girlfriend of hers who had a daughter around my age, which was 16 at the time, and you made my mother laugh harder than I had ever heard her laugh. And she needed it. Bill, my father walked out on my mother and sisters and me, leaving her to be both "America's Mom and Dad" and she pulled it off. She got herself a job, dropped us off at a babysitter's, sometimes before the sun had come up, and then, often after the sun had set, picked us up, drove home, cooked dinner, supervised baths, sometimes combining the two, plunking the three of us in the tub together, and feeding us Campbell's soup from a pot.

"One spoon for you, one for you, one for you," and on and on until the pot was empty and we were clean.

Weekends were spent doing laundry, cleaning the house, and taking care of the yards, front and back.

She did it all. She rewarded herself with a vodka tonic or glass of wine while sitting in her girlfriend's kitchen when possible. She dated once in a while, but really, who wants to get involved with a woman who has three kids under the age of 10.

And she did all this while my father was building a Spanish villa on a hillside in one of those one percent communities that smart kids visit on Halloween. He even began collecting purebred horses for weekend adventures. When he wasn't off flying his own plane.

I digress. Sorry.

As I look back, I can't imagine where my mother got the strength. But she did.

I don't recall who came up with the idea of driving up to Lake Tahoe for a night at a fancy casino. I have no idea where we got the money. Travel of any kind was not something we did. But I recall with clarity, sitting in one of those curved, tufted, red leather booths in a crowded room with waiters and waitresses coming around and taking our orders. My mother was dressed up! She had a brocade frock in greens and gold. Her hair was in a French twist. She wore earrings and a necklace. She didn't smoke, but her friend did, which I believed to be the height of glamour. Her friend had large breasts, which I was embarrassed by. She showed an abundance of cleavage. My mother's dress had what is known as a "boat neck." No cleavage to be seen. She must have only been in her mid-30's.

My mother ordered a vodka tonic for herself and a Shirley Temple for me. Her friend drank martinis. I was impressed by the wide glass and the fragile-looking stem. I had not seen one before and was intrigued by a drink with olives in it. Order enough of them and you could call it dinner! It seemed as efficient as soup in the bathtub.

We knew you from your television show, "I Spy". And my neighbor, Mike, had one of your albums. You were young and handsome and funny as fuck.

You were alone on the stage, in the spotlight. You had a chair you used as a prop for a bit about driving on the hills in San Francisco. My mother laughed until she cried. She laughed loud and hard. I had never seen her cut loose like that.

Her face was lit up, her blue eyes danced and filled with tears from laughing. She grabbed my hand at one point and looked me deep in my eyes and grinned. It was the first time I saw my mother as a young woman rather than a tired, overworked mom.

You gave her that. You provided a time and place for her to let go.

It would be the only time I took a trip with my mother, just us. There would be family vacations with my cousins once or twice. But this, this was a trip for my mother and me. We shared a room in the hotel, something we had never done before and have never done since.

My mother is still alive, but has no memory of that vacation. I have asked her, but so much of her memory bank has been wiped clean by time. She resides in an assisted living facility where not many of her companions remember much about their thirties, I'm sure. At least not judging from the conversations we try to have around the dining table at lunch, surrounded by walkers and wheelchairs.

I sit beside my mother and watch as she enjoys a glass of lemonade and her coffee with two creams. She has great recall when it comes to my father leaving her. I wish she didn't. Sometimes she tells me he has come to visit her. I remind her that he died years ago. She shakes her head and swears she just saw him.

She cries a lot of the time. I have tried to prime the pump when it comes to recalling good times in the past. But as I have said, when I mention you, she has a blank expression. Perhaps that's better, given how things have turned out.

One of your accusers has stated that it was in the 1960s that you raped her. She claims it took place in a hotel at Lake Tahoe. Small world, huh?

So, here we are. You are despicable. And yet I thank you for that one night so many years ago. I was able to see in my mother a young, beautiful, vibrant woman who seemed to be without a care in the world. You gave her that. I'm just grateful you didn't invite her backstage after the show.

You disgust me, you filthy pig.

Claudia

Bill (William) Henry Cosby Jr. was born in 1937. He is a comedian, actor, writer, musician and convicted rapist. He now lives in prison.

Once thought of as "America's Dad", I now think of him as a narcissistic, pathological liar who preyed on women.

Don't bother watching any of his past work or reading any of his books.

Dear Ray Charles,

Not to be rude, but you had the skinniest legs I think I have ever seen on a grown man. You were wearing a baby blue tuxedo, and descending the old wooden steps in the shade of the full and leafy oak trees in Aptos Village Park. You looked as rickety as the stairs you were navigating with the help of a curvaceous young woman much younger than I. I wanted her job!

I also wanted to run up and greet you and tell you how much I appreciated you. Not just for your music, but for teaching me about the relationship a man could have with a woman. A husband with a wife. Growing up with no man in the house, I was without a clue.

Security, however, was present, and I fully understood that they would not welcome me with open arms. I did move up from the 10th row, where I had been sitting, to the second row where I found a vacant seat. I only needed a single, as I had stayed home to hang with you rather than go away for the weekend with my husband and our friends to a lovely house by a lake.

For years, the small village of Aptos has hosted a music festival over the Memorial Day Weekend. When I saw that you would be headlining, I decided that I would forego the three days by the lake with my husband and pals so that I might finally see you in the flesh. I'm getting old, you are much older, how many more chances might I get? And the park is within walking distance from my house. The only thing better would have been to find you singing in my front yard, the entire orchestra, including the Raelettes, backing you. But that was not going to happen.

In the days leading up to your arrival, I listened to your music constantly. It took me right back to Oakland and the small house I grew up in with my mother and younger sisters. My mother did not play your music. She was more an Andy Williams, Johnny Mathis gal. My neighbors across the street played your albums with wonderful regularity. The husband and wife could be found dancing in the living room, and as I recall they were often wearing their thick, white terrycloth bathrobes, which makes me wonder what I was doing there.

I was mesmerized by their behavior. There was more going on than meets the eye, I was sure. But just what it was, I didn't yet understand. Only as I grew older did I realize that the energy in that living room was sexual. Again, why was I there? In any case, your voice hinted at a world I had yet to experience. It was mysterious and exciting.

Andy Williams did not have the same effect on me. Neither did Johnny Mathis. And I mean no disrespect.

The music festival is a giant party on the green. Booths are set up selling drinks, food, CDs, and whatever else might tempt the concertgoers. You were scheduled to go on at the end of the day. It had been a warm afternoon and lots of folks put away lots of beer and wine and some who had been seated in the front rows simply wandered off as you were making your way to the stage. (I was so very glad you could not see them!)

Thus, my advance to the front.

You brought everyone with you to our little park. The entire orchestra, all in their tuxes. The luscious Raelettes radiating sexuality with their sultry voices. I had to pinch myself. It is an odd thing to see someone so close up after imagining them for so long. As you began to sing "Georgia on My Mind", I pictured my neighbors all those decades back, sliding around on the hardwood floors in their white socks, in their white robes, locked in their own mysterious world. I thought they represented everything my own household was lacking. A man, a woman, love, sex, passion.

A few months after that concert in the park, you died. And not long after that, I heard a story about my long-ago neighbors. It seems the husband had an entire second family hidden away in an apartment in downtown Oakland. I don't know if the wife ever knew,

but I tend to believe she would have to have had suspicions. The last I heard, both have dementia and are still together and being cared for.

I wish I could visit them. I'd put on one of your records and see if they'd react. I like to think they would. I like to imagine them shuffling across the floor in each other's arms, locked in a romantic moment which, in reality, may never have actually existed.

Your fan,
Claudia

Ray Charles Robinson was born in 1930 and died in 2004. He was an American musician, singer and writer of songs. He began to lose his eyesight at the age of 5 and, by the age of 7, was blind. From all accounts, he did not let that slow him down. The man could sing. And play. And party.

My knees still get wobbly when I listen to him sing "Georgia".

Dear Mort Sahl,

I used to cut school to watch you on the "Merv Griffin Show". I was an odd kid. I was simply determined to set you up with my mother. I wanted you to meet her, fall in love, marry her and move on in with the Nielsen girls.

As an adult, I now realize that was a ridiculous notion. My mother, sweet, kind, hardworking, exhausted all of the time, would not have had the energy to even have a five-minute conversation with you. Especially if you got on to one of your rants about conspiracies, the Kennedys, the Vietnam War, or even the price of tea in China, an expression my mother used often, which I never quite got.

She would have gotten up from the kitchen table while you were still pontificating, put the dishes into the soapy water, called each of her daughters in to help clean up, and then gone off to bed with a movie magazine to keep her company. You, I imagine, would still be performing at the chrome dinette set lounge.

But still.

What if you did meet? And there was a tiny spark? And even if I were the only one who noticed, I could fan it into a flame. Our lives would change!

We would move to a house in the Berkeley Hills. We would have floor to ceiling bookshelves, filled. We would have threadbare oriental carpets on the hardwood floors. You would sit in your leather easy chair in the evenings, teaching me things I didn't even realize I wanted to know!

There would be a fireplace. With a roaring fire! Wood stacked in a bin next to it. On the nights you were performing in the clubs across the bay, you would invite me along.

While my mother read her movie magazines in bed in Berkeley, I would sit on a special reserved bar stool sipping Shirley Temples and watching your act. We would have a secret signal and you would use it often to let me know you could see me. To let me know that you were so happy I was there witnessing your brilliant monologue. Which I understood completely.

Such a clever girl!

Then we would drive back home together, me falling asleep mid-span of the Bay Bridge. You would ease me out of the car and carry me up the stairs to the front door. I would pretend to be asleep, because it was perfect. Inside, the fire in the fireplace would be down to embers, glowing in the dark. The lights from the San Francisco skyline would twinkle in the distance.

Down the hall you would carry me, depositing me on my bed in My Own Room! Only after I heard you close the door would I open my eyes fully. Then close them again, not wanting the dream to end.

Can you imagine, Mort?

Xo,
Claudia

Morton Lyon Sahl was born in Canada in 1927. Known as a stand-up comedian he was renowned for his biting political satire. Anyone and everyone was a target.

I finally got to see him live at a club in San Francisco, the hungry i, in the 1970s. My old pal Pete the Pilot took me. (Thanks Pete!)

Mort also did his share of film work and appeared often on television, especially the above mentioned Merv Griffin Show.

Do I now need to tell you who Merv Griffin is? YouTube him.

On October 26, 2021, Mort Sahl died quietly in his home in Mill Valley, California at the age of 94.

Dear Henry Clay Frick,

I love going to your mansion on Fifth Ave. Thank you for turning it into a museum for anyone willing to pay to enjoy. Standing in what was your library and gazing out the curtains to the bustling street outside, I try to imagine what it must have been like to stand in that exact spot decades ago and watch horses and carriages pass by. It is odd to think that one might hear the clip clop of hooves and perhaps get a whiff of the leavings of said horses while surrounded by such luxuries as there are in this room.

I have treated myself to visits to your former home countless times and have always wanted to explore it further. To go beyond the velvet ropes, which strongly suggest to the curious that we need to respect the boundaries in place. No peeking into some of the more private areas of the mansion. However, one day not long ago, I was invited by one of the staff members to explore your home more fully than I ever had before.

New York City is the place I go to find whatever it seems to be I am missing in life. And a few years ago, I was missing my sister terribly. I was missing them both, actually. But one had died, and the other, her twin, had somehow slipped through my fingers. Only a few weeks after the funeral of the one who had passed, I was on a plane and headed to New York to search for something I couldn't even name. Happiness seemed to be asking for too much. Unbridled joy seemed utterly unattainable. Peace perhaps?

Jose, the doorman, greeted me upon my arrival. His embrace was warm and his chocolate brown, wool uniform jacket scratchy, but oddly comforting.

Once upstairs and tucked into to my borrowed apartment, I wandered room to room before settling on a bar stool in the kitchen where I drank tequila and watched the sky shift from deep purple to dark blue to black. Snow was predicted for the next day and, sure enough, when, in the middle of the night, I woke to that soft, thick silence which accompanies a snow fall, I returned to my perch by the window and watched as the fat flakes fell silently outside. Returning to bed, I felt as though I was wrapped in a cocoon. I slept deeply.

I wonder, Mr. Frick, if you ever stood at the window in your library and watched the snow come down. Did you ever slip out the front door and cross the avenue for a midnight walk in the park, your boots crunching on the fresh-fallen snow? Your footprints disappearing in moments, as if you had not passed by. I hope you did. The park in all of its winter glory is a sight to be remembered.

In the morning, after coffee and a raspberry scone, I layered up to venture outside. I wore black. Black leggings and a black cashmere sweater, a black down coat, and black cashmere gloves, and watch cap. Jose was on the door. He warned me about the temperature outside. I'm not going far, I told him. Just to The Frick.

The streets had been cleared, but the snow kept falling. There seemed to be few people out walking and, those who were, were smart enough to carry umbrellas. I was not as prepared. By the time I reached your house, my nose was running and my hat was soaked. I didn't mind though, it seemed appropriate given my mood. Soggy, sad, and rather broken.

A kind friend had introduced me to a staff member, who is employed by the Frick Collection. She met me at the entrance and was gracious enough not to notice my disheveled appearance. I stuffed my hat into my pocket and she offered to hang up my coat to be retrieved later.

The two of us wandered room to room. "Girl with a Pearl Earring" was on loan from its home in Amsterdam, and I was able to stand alone in front of it for what seemed like hours. But while enjoying the masterpiece, I kept thinking about my sisters. Years earlier, they had accompanied me to New York to see a collection of Dutch masters at the Metropolitan Museum. I had given my sister Cheryl a copy of the novel, "Girl with a Pearl Earring", by Tracy Chevalier to read so she might become more familiar with the painting and develop an emotional attachment to it, even though the book is fiction.

Feeling the loss of both siblings, I stepped away from the painting and continued on.

We had covered everything there was to see in the public areas of your home, when my tour guide asked if I wanted to see what was downstairs. She invited me to step beyond the velvet rope. I eagerly took the bait.

Well, count me as being gobsmacked! A bowling alley? Mr. Frick, you have a bowling alley in your basement! A humdinger! Beautiful hardwood lanes, two of them! Balls waiting in the ball return. Pins all set up!

My host invited me to bowl a few. I picked up a ball and placed my fingers in the holes and thought about who may have been the last person to try to knock down a few pins. You, Mr. Frick? The missus? A Vanderbilt or Morgan?

The possibilities were endless. I asked.

"Well, the last person to use the bowling alley was Woody Allen," she said. Okay, I'm good with that.

I knocked down a few. Then rolled again and knocked down some more. There was no automatic pin setter, so I immediately panicked. What was the etiquette here? What does one do when one has knocked down Mr. Frick's bowling pins and there is no machine to prop them back up?

I asked.

"We have people," she replied. Of course you do, Mr. Frick.

I began to laugh. It echoed through the basement. The sound startled me. At first, I tried to suppress it. Guilt set in immediately. How could I laugh? My sister was gone. Both were gone. But then I recalled long ago Saturday afternoons when my father would come visit and take us bowling and how much they loved it. How they won trophies for their skill. And I thought how much they would have loved seeing this. Doing this.

Bowling in your basement with the "Girl with a Pearl Earring" hanging right upstairs. Really, sublime.

So, Mr. Frick, I thank you. You gave me a break in my mourning. You enabled me to feel my sisters. To imagine them with me rolling those heavy balls towards those spindly pins. They would have thrown strikes. I would not have minded if they cleaned my clock. It was a spectacular adventure. It only could have been improved upon by my sisters actually being there to share the experience.

Perhaps they were.

Sincerely,
Claudia

Henry Clay Frick was born in 1849 in Pennsylvania and died in 1919. If I had been alive then, I doubt our paths would have crossed. He was an industrialist, financier, art-patron and, sadly, a union buster. According to those who have followed his career, he wasn't above firing a gun into a crowd of union organizers to bust up the gathering. He funded the construction of the Pennsylvania Railroad, and was a member of the South Fork Fishing and Hunting Club, which doesn't really impress me.

Go ahead and Google him. Read about his involvement in the Johnstown Flood. As our current president would say, "Not Good."

But man, could he collect art. His Fifth Avenue mansion has been turned into a museum and anyone with a credit card or a few bucks in their pocket may go inside and check out how the 1% lived back in the day.

Dear Woody Allen,

We have not met. Although I have seen you often walking down Lexington Avenue, in the neighborhood I call my home away from home. You do not seem like a man who would enjoy a friendly hello offered up on the street by a perfect (oh, who am I kidding, I am far from perfect) stranger. So, I just keep on going. I will say, however, I have imagined you stopping me and saying hello. Just because I have become a familiar face, and you are beginning to feel silly and slightly embarrassed that you recognize me, but can't quite place me. Then you would invite me over for a beer and some baseball watching on television. I have heard that watching the All-American Past Time is one of your favorite activities.

Okay, I know you have issues. Baggage. Some people have written you off, what with your colorful family history. But, let me say for the record, if I believed all that was said, I would not be writing you a thank you note. So, I am not even going to get into the more salacious accusations. I do believe that the young woman who has accused you of terrible things truly believes you did them. I am not convinced.

You did marry someone who might have been called inappropriate, though. I mean, we all know that she wasn't actually your daughter, you were not related to her, but really? Kind of icky-ish at first glance. I can totally see why Mia would be pissed. But selfishly, I loved it.

You took the heat off of me. You may wonder why.

My father, quite like you in many ways, also made some creative choices when it came to lifetime partners. While married to my mother, he struck up an affair with my mother's good friend. And, to add to the fun, the woman, Ellie, was also the wife of his law partner. She even worked in the office. I assume my father was getting a bit bored with his life, married, three kids, and wanted to add a little spice, some excitement, but was a little too lazy to go out and see what was available. So, he just stepped out of his office, saw Ellie sitting at her desk wearing a red dress and smoking a cigarette and bingo!

It ruined the relationship my mother had with Ellie. Didn't do much for my mom and dad's relationship either. And the law partnership...well, just imagine.

Ellie and my dad married. I offered to be the flower girl, but the offer was declined. I was bummed. At seven years old, I thought pitching rose petals out of a basket while strolling down the aisle in front of the bride was something I was born to do. Apparently, it was not. My invitation must have gotten lost in the mail.

They stayed married for a decade or so, but then my father got restless once again.

Perhaps his ego needed boosting. Perhaps he was simply swept off his feet by the beautiful young woman, and she too was swept away with love and could not resist. But, once again, my father did not go out into the world to find love; he did not go far at all.

Ellie had invited her niece, Bonnie, and Bonnie's husband to come for a visit. They brought their two children, both not much more than babies. When I was invited to visit, I began to think of Bonnie as a cousin. We had family dinners. We drank too much. My father, an avid horseman at the time, signed up for weekend endurance races and Bonnie, Ellie, and I, along with various other family members and friends, would go along. And again, lots of drinking.

Rumors began to fly. Accusations were made. Ellie threw dishes. A gun was fired. The family, once again, was in chaos.

Then my father married Bonnie. Ellie, like Mia, was pissed. I mean, her husband had married her niece. Once again, he stuck close to home when it came to switching things up. Eventually, we all got used to the idea and life went on. Now, when I am with a group of people and someone asks me about my family history, I don't think of it being as ground-breaking as it once was. And that is thanks to you.

"He married his daughter," I hear people say when they talk about you and Soon-Yi. And I am quick to point out that, in fact, you did not. And then I go on to say that, if they are going by the fact that at one time your now wife was "like" a daughter to you, then I have to apply the same ill-founded logic to my own family and say that my father married my mother's best friend only to leave her for his niece. Which is almost correct, but if looked at closely, is not true at all.

What is with you guys? How lazy can you be? Would it have been too much to ask that you venture out of your own family to find your new partner? Someone you have not been exchanging birthday and Christmas gifts with for years? Although now that I think of it, it is nice that no new names needed to be added to the annual gift exchange.

Oh, dear Woody, you have made me feel as if I am not the only person on the planet with a colorful family history. I thank you for that.

Maybe next time I see you in the hood, I'll reach out and give you a high five. And then I'll just keep going, respecting your need for privacy even though, like my father, you really did bring a lot of the attention on yourself!

Warm regards,
Claudia

P.S. How about that Frick bowling alley?!

Heywood "Woody" Allen was born in 1935. A writer, director, actor, stand-up comedian, and musician, he began writing jokes and scripts in the 1950s. Many of his earlier films were wacky, slapstick affairs which didn't really appeal to me. But then here came Annie Hall, Manhattan, *and* Hanna and Her Sisters, *and I was over the moon.* Midnight in Paris *and* Blue Jasmine *are also real gems.*

As I have said, his personal life has been, at times, a sticky mess.

He can often be found playing his clarinet with his band, New Orleans Jazz Band, at the Carlyle Hotel in Manhattan. He may also be spotted walking, hatted-head down, on Lexington Ave.

Dear Jerry Garcia,

Thank you for helping me get the chance to experience the most moan-inducing, toe-curling sex I have ever had.

I suppose I should also thank the rest of the band, but really, you were the draw. The hook. And I will confess I took you all for granted.

Growing up and living in Oakland, and then Berkeley, it seemed as though The Grateful Dead were playing every weekend, to the point where I had little or no idea that you were more than just a local band.

Excusez-moi!

I was not a "follower" or a Dead Head, so what you were up to when you weren't in my neck of the woods was not on my radar.

Then I met Michael, who I believe moved to California because of you. Oh, he claims it was because he had an older brother who lived in Berkeley, but he also has an older brother living in New Jersey, so something tipped the scales. And I do believe it was you.

His Berkeley brother was a Dead Head from way back. To this day, his garage is filled with concert memorabilia. Michael has told me about the first day he arrived in town, driving his beater of a Mustang, and saw a poster saying that you would be playing that very night.

Who knew that heaven was just 3,000 miles from New Jersey?! But for my husband, it was. He probably made the entire cross-country trip listening to you! He was fresh out of college and looking for adventure. You were his soundtrack. Our paths crossed.

Actually, I hired him. He was adorable and, while I don't want to sound inappropriate now that we are fully aware of what should and should not be done in the workplace, I was quite taken with his glossy brown ponytail and his winning smile.

I worked at a pool and tennis club, and we needed to hire a "pool boy" to set up the lounge chairs every morning and act as lifeguard in the afternoons. It was the end of summer and our other "kids" had to return to school.

Here came Michael, looking for a job.

He was smart, could work a 40-hour week with no problem, had a degree in business, which he would not be using in this particular profession, and didn't mind arriving at the crack of dawn to open the pool and soon, I discovered, enjoyed making a fresh pot of coffee, which would be waiting for me when I arrived.

And, as I said, adorable.

First, it was just making the coffee. Then we graduated to him pouring me a mug and delivering it to my desk. Then he would deliver the coffee and ever-so-briefly place one hand on my shoulder.

One morning, while driving to the club, I realized I was really looking forward to that touch. Almost as much as the coffee.

Soon, I began to look forward to the touch even more than the coffee. "He likes you," other employees stated, grinning.

"Don't be ridiculous," I always replied. I was his boss.

I was eight years older.

I was divorced and had no desire to get in some inappropriate relationship. I was happy being single and living my own life and blah, blah, blah. I planned on never having sex again because it always got complicated.

So there.

For his 22nd birthday, I bought him a loaf of cinnamon bread from the bakery across the street from the club. They tied the end of the cellophane bag with a brown and white checked ribbon.

He ate the bread and tied the ribbon onto his rearview mirror in the beat-up Mustang. He asked me to walk with him to the parking lot so he could show me. Then he asked me if I would go with him over to Marin on Saturday and have a picnic and a hike.

"Just as friends," he said.

"I just don't know my way around there," he continued.

"I swear to god if you tell anyone at work, I will fire you," I countered.

It was not a sunny day. Rain threatened as we drove over the San Rafael Bridge, listening to you the entire way, and, by the time we parked in the Marin Headlands and began our hike, the rain hit hard and heavy.

I did not want to seem like an old fuddy-duddy who couldn't get wet, so off we went. We had backpacks filled with food and a bottle of wine and as we made our way a tension began to build. Sexual. For real.

We came to a downed tree and decided to take a break and sat next to each other on the old Redwood. Rain was pattering. Birds had all gone into hiding. There were no other hikers around. It was cold. I believe he asked me if I wanted him to put his arm around me to try to warm me up.

Or I may have just moved in on him …

Oh, Jerry. It was so cozy. We huddled under his jacket and began to make out like teenagers, which he almost still was, and, in no time, I was amazingly warm. Hot.

Before it was too late, I came to my senses, and said I was very hungry for the sharp cheddar cheese and whole wheat crackers we had packed. He peeled an orange and divided the segments, and I swear that to this day the smell of citrus has an erotic effect on me.

We straightened our clothes and tried to act as if no boundaries had been crossed. But they had. I mean, we hadn't "done it," but it was close.

I couldn't undo the things we had done, but I could take charge of the situation and make damn sure it didn't happen again!

Then we got back to the car. The warm, dry little hideaway with the ribbon hanging from the mirror and your music in the tape player.

I was a mature, professional woman who was Not Looking for Romance.

There was a small movie theater in an old Quonset hut in one of the little towns in Marin County. As we were passing by, I noticed that an Alfred Hitchcock movie was playing. "The 39 Steps". Fearing (hoping?), what might happen if we just stayed in the car, I suggested we park and go in.

As the movie played, I was so aware of him sitting next to me I had no idea what was going on in the film.

He held my hand. He rubbed the palm of my hand with his thumb. The lights came up and I was positive that every person in the makeshift theater knew exactly what we were thinking. Or, in my case, trying not to think about.

It took about an hour to get back home to Berkeley. Michael did not even ask if I wanted to go to my house. He drove straight to his house (where, eventually, I would live with him), and offered to make me a pot of tea. Nice herbal tea for a cold, wet night. Organic honey to go with.

He had housemates, so we took the tea up to his bedroom. Well, Jerry, we never drank the tea.

He massaged my shoulders, massaged my feet! Claimed I deserved it after all of the hiking and lugging a backpack.

He scratched my back, an activity that I believe should always be included in foreplay. Our damp clothes mingled on the floor as we mingled in the bed.

It felt, without trying to sound like a romance novel, like he had awakened something in me that had been dormant. It was spectacular. I am not kidding.

This kid was talented! Was every male in New Jersey this gifted? We made a pact to keep it all a secret. No one at work could ever know.

Difficult once we began to live together.

Now, 35 years later, you are long gone, and we are still together. I believe Michael misses you more than I do. But I also believe that I am the most grateful to you and the rest of the Dead.

You brought me Michael. He brought me back to life.

Keep on Truckin',
Claudia

Jerry Garcia was born in 1942 and died in 1995. He was the lead guitarist for the band The Grateful Dead for 30 years. And, I believe, with all of the extremely hard partying, that, actually, is more like 60 years. Being a Deadhead, a follower of the band, became an entire counter-culture movement.

Jerry's been gone for years, and Grateful Dead cover bands still pack bars all around the country. There's one in my neighborhood that plays every Sunday evening at a local bar. But they take into account the average age of a fan of Jerry, and their first set begins at 5:30 in the evening.

Tie dye is required.

Dear O.J. Simpson,

So, you're out. Well, at least you did spend a bit of time behind bars. Not fucking enough in my opinion, but no one asked me what I thought so, whatever. Despite the fact that I do believe you committed two vicious murders, I am writing to thank you.

Years before you slit the throats of two innocent people, you and I met. And, because of you, I was able to spend three days in Los Angeles with my sister, Carol. We stayed at the Disneyland Hotel, because, why not?

I'll back up just a bit.

My younger sister and I ran a tennis shop at a small club in Northern California. Carol was the brains of the outfit. She could figure out how many cases of tennis balls we would need for the year. She could run a tournament like an army drill sergeant. She managed the payroll and paid the bills. Fashion, however, was not her strong suit. That is where I would step in and take over. Together we made a good team.

Oh, I think she could have tackled it all if need be. But she made a place for me in that little shop and I deeply

appreciated it. I worked by her side before I got married.
While I was married. And after said marriage hit the skids.
The tennis club was more home to me than anywhere. My
sister my most reliable partner. I think she had similar
feelings towards me, as our other sister, Cheryl, her twin, was
living in Peru and was, I am sure, deeply missed by Carol.

Early in the morning, we would open the shop for
the before-work players. Late in the day, we would sit at
the bar upstairs and drink with the after-work players.
During the day, we would take turns taking breaks to
head out to the courts and play. One more area in which
she was the master, I the student. And every now and
then, we would discuss the merits of "going to market."
Traveling to wherever market was being held to take a
look at what was new in tennis. Oversized rackets, the
latest in footwear and cutting-edge tennis togs. We
always had to take into account the expense in traveling
versus staying home and phoning in orders or waiting
for a sales rep to come to us.

When we first received the information about the
spring market to be held in Los Angeles, she was
hesitant to sign up. It would be a nine- or ten-hour
drive, or we would need to fly. A hotel would have to be
booked for three nights. There would be meals to buy
and all manner of unexpected expenses.

Sure, there would also be tennis stars sitting at
tables with their sponsors, but we had both seen our
share of tennis players.

The brochures sat on the counter of the store for
days while we debated. Carol was leaning towards not

going. I didn't want to force the issue, but I was longing for a mini-vacation, and we had never traveled alone together before.

Then I noticed something in the information packet. You, Orenthal James Simpson, would be there. O.J., in the house!

I pointed it out to Carol. Our eyes locked and she grinned. She was a fan. That's all it took. She was in!

We threw caution to the wind and bought airline tickets. We booked a double room at Disneyland's hotel. We had room service; one of her favorite things. She ordered a strawberry daiquiri with extra whipped cream. I drank tequila. We lay on the bed and watched movies at night and, during the day, wandered booth to booth looking at merchandise.

We met Ilie Nastase at the Adidas booth and were not impressed. He was slimy, asking me to "come sit on his lap," which I did not do. But we did order shoes.

Then we spotted you sitting at a table pimping yourself out. I'm sorry to say I can't, for the life of me, remember what you were promoting. But we queued up to meet you and, once at the front of the line, you first greeted Carol, reaching out to shake her hand and smiling. Then it was my turn. I remember how big your hand was. Mine disappeared into it. I remember how beautiful your smile was. I recall wondering how a football player could have such perfect teeth.

And your forehead was so shiny, the overhead lights creating a halo effect. We got autographs. I have no idea what happened to them.

That was the only time I ever took a trip alone with Carol. It only happened because you were going to be there. Those three days seem like a dream to me now. Cheryl moved back from Peru. She and Carol picked up where they left off, twins, forever joined.

The tennis shop was sold years ago. We three went on to other life adventures, Carol and Cheryl still with their unshakeable bond until Carol's death just a few years ago. I wish I could say that Cheryl then turned to me for sisterly companionship, but that was not the case. Somehow, I lost both sisters in one fell swoop.

But I have the memories of that trip. Those three days in the Magic Kingdom with my brilliant, funny, talented sister. A time I know I wouldn't have had if not for you.

Now while I firmly believe you are a monster who should never be forgiven (after all, how does one forgive someone who refuses to admit their guilt), I do thank you. For those three days back in the 1970s. Before you murdered the mother of your children and her innocent friend. Before we were all were mesmerized by the white Ford Bronco chase. Before I could even imagine the pain of losing two sisters: one to cancer, the other to an unexpected turn of events.

So, as much as I hate to say it, thank you, you murdering piece of shit.

Sincerely,
Claudia

Orenthal James Simpson was born in 1947. He attended USC and played football for the USC Trojans, winning the Heisman Trophy in 1968. He was a pretty great football player, but ended up being a pretty horrible individual. After years of professional football, he became known for running through airports in television commercials for a rental car company and for playing a lot of golf. Then he became famous for riding in the back of a white Ford Bronco while the police chased him after his ex-wife and a friend were found murdered in her own front yard.

He was not found guilty. W.T.F.?

He did go to prison later for armed robbery and kidnapping. After getting out, he retreated back to the golf course and swears he is still looking for his ex-wife's murderer.

Dear Oprah,

Sometimes I wonder if you had been given a more common name, Joan, Letty, Fran, would you then need to use your last name? It is one thing to have a name so singular that one may just go by it, but another if your name is more Plain Jane. I wonder if your mother had some kind of premonition when she gave you that moniker or if, as I have heard, it was a case of misspelling a biblical name.

Well, whatever, it seems to be working just fine for you. And as they say, if it ain't broke don't fix it!

Still, perhaps my salutation should be more formal: *Dear Ms. Winfrey,*

A few years ago, you were waiting in line at a deli in Santa Barbara just like any other local. You may have gone unnoticed by the regulars, or at least they were keeping a respectful distance while your sandwich was being constructed, but one woman could not stop herself from saying hello. My sister, Carol, who loved you as much as she loved sandwiches, which was a lot.

Apparently, Carol's twin, Cheryl, was distracted by the delectable goodies in the display case, because she was unaware of your presence. She didn't look up when Carol, after introducing herself to you, whispered loudly, "Cheryl."

"Cheryl, Cheryl, CHERYL!"

Finally, you stepped in, Ms. Winfrey, and with a sly smile said, "Cheryl?" and got her attention.

Cheryl may or may not have wet her pants. She has never said.

You were so kind, Ms. Winfrey. You chatted while the sandwiches were built. You offered to have seats set aside for one of your shows and gave Carol the name of the woman in charge of tickets. You gave her the phone number!

Minutes later Carol called me from the car. "Guess who we just met?" she asked me.

"Well, kind of a wide range of options," I told her. "Give me a clue."

Santa Barbara. Sandwiches. Famous. I wasn't getting it quickly enough for my efficient sister.

"OPRAH!" she declared.

And now, Carol said, get a pen and paper. Write this down. Call this woman. Get us all tickets!

My sister was afraid if we didn't move on this opportunity ASAP it might just disappear. A bubble burst.

So, I did just that. Made the call, secured the tickets, and began to imagine a trip to Chicago with my sisters. We would stay at a grand hotel. We would order room service. We would take a cab to "The Oprah Winfrey Show", where seats would be waiting for us!

Oh please, maybe it would be one of her giveaway shows!!! You get a pony, you get a pony, you get a pony!!!

It was just a few weeks later that Carol called me again. To tell me about the cancer. Real cancer this time. Not a strange lump in the neck, but cancer of the esophagus, which looked as if it may not be fixable.

In the end, we had to turn down your generous invitation to visit you in the Windy City. You did send her an autographed picture, which I thought was kind. She taped it to her bedroom mirror. In the months that followed, it was joined by get-well cards and letters from friends and family. Almost a full year went by, filled with treatments, surgeries, terror, anger, love, and a fighting will so strong that my sister survived and lived another twelve years before cancer returned and took her with lightning speed.

I don't know where the photo is now. But I do know the joy that meeting you brought to her. And the gift of imagining a trip to Chicago gave us all a thrill. I sometimes fantasize about what that trip might have been. The adventure of seeing a new city with my sisters. Of feeling the excitement, of being in the audience as you walked out onto the stage.

Oh, Oprah (may I call you that now that you know who I am?), what a gift you gave her. Gave us.

You get a wish. You get a wish. You get a wish!

We, none of us, needed a new pony really. The kindness, the granting of a wish to go to your show, that was plenty.

I know Carol would agree.

In gratitude,
Claudia

Oprah Winfrey was born in 1954. She began her career as a television personality on a local station in Tennessee. She then went on to host her own talk show, which was so hugely successful that she no longer needed her last name. OPRAH had officially landed on the planet. From 1986 until 2011, when she retired from her show, it often felt as if she were queen of the universe. It still does.

I mean really, why am I telling you who Oprah is? Everyone knows.

Dear David Blaine,

First, I think you are nuts! Who decides to make a living sitting on flag poles or trapped in ice for ridiculous amounts of time?

Why would someone want to live in a giant fish bowl in Lincoln Center for, what was it, a week? But, thanks!

There is never a shortage of things to do in New York City. It is one of the great perks of spending time in Manhattan. So, while I am there for months at a time, I try to keep abreast of what is going on. Free museum days. Free concerts in the parks and churches. Outdoor movies under the stars. Shakespeare in the Park. The sample chocolates they give out at the Lindt store on Fifth Avenue. Actually, any of their candy emporiums.

Curled up in my bed one night watching the news, I was intrigued by one of the last stories of the evening. On the screen was the beautiful fountain in front of Lincoln Centre. In front of the fountain was a large tank. I can only describe it as a fishbowl. It would be, according to the reporter, your home for the next week or so. You would be plopping yourself in the next day. And there you would remain for all the passing world to see. I contemplated this news. I wondered if someone could actually do that. Live in a giant bowl of water for a week. I wondered why they might want to.

Boils down to money, I suppose. Or, as I said up top, you are nuts. Or, a third option, once you think up a challenge, you then decide you simply have to go for it. Curiosity wins out.

In the morning, I decided to take a walk before settling in at my desk. My desk, located in my temporary home, was only a few blocks from Lincoln Centre. So what the hell? Why not check out the action?

As I arrived, I saw that a small bank of bleachers had been set up and the large, water- filled sphere sat in the sun. Other than the water, it was empty.

There were people standing around with microphones and cables were stretched across the plaza. I moved to the back side of the fishbowl and watched as nothing really went on. I had neglected to look up any information about this underwater performance, so didn't know when the starting pistol was supposed to sound.

But the weather was perfect and there was a vendor selling pastries and coffee, so, as far as I could see, so far so good.

There was a slight commotion behind me, and I turned around just as you and your "people" approached.

You looked me in the eye, may I say you have quite an impressive gaze, and reached out and took my hand and shook it and thanked me for coming out.

You then climbed up the ladder that led to the top of the bowl, waved to the crowd in front, and, after adjusting your diving helmet, lowered yourself into the water.

People cheered. They took turns walking up a small ramp which was placed directly in front of the glass tank. You watched them. You placed your hands on the glass, so they might place theirs against yours. For a public event, it felt very intimate. You would be fed by tubes. I have no idea what you would do for bathroom breaks.

You became part of my daily walks. Sometimes mornings, often evenings. You were never alone. Curious well-wishers were always there. Walking the ramp, placing their hands, walking back down.

Sometimes you made faces. Sometimes you just looked exhausted.

I am not a sound sleeper. I wake often. That week, I would lie in bed and wonder how you were getting along just blocks away. I was often tempted to go see. To make sure you were okay. It was an odd feeling to think about you in real time, just floating in your Upper West Side pool.

You were still in your bath when I packed up my bags and flew back to California. My husband and I watched you leave your underwater home on our television from the comfort of our couch. You were not in good shape. You were actually lifted out rather than climbing out on your own.

Some say you actually failed your underwater experiment. I say that not drowning or losing your mind means this was a rousing success. It was a sort of magic. How else to explain the fact that one man in a bowl of water could attract so much attention for a full week? You brought together people from all backgrounds, all political affiliations, and all different religions for seven days. You made us, me anyway, forget about any problems we might have had.

We watched, cheered, clapped, and pulled for you to succeed. No matter what personal histories or baggage we brought to the plaza, they all fell away as we stood witness to a crazy/brave/curious man attempting to do what should be impossible for no reason I could think of. Unless that was your goal. Which perhaps it was. We could use a lot more of this kind of magic.

For this, I thank you.

Swimmingly yours,
Claudia

David Blaine was born in 1973. I suppose we should call him an illusionist. He has made the Statue of Liberty "disappear." He has lived frozen in a block of ice for days.

He had himself buried in a plastic box for seven days and lived to tell about it. Harry Houdini's niece was there when Blaine emerged from said box and stated her uncle could never have pulled off the trick. High praise!

And if you don't know who Harry is, Google. YouTube. He was also quite the trickster.

Dear Carrie Bradshaw,

I am fully aware that you do not actually exist. Oh, I can binge watch you on HBO, and I can reread the book that gave birth to the popular television show and movies, but you are fiction. Life for most residents of New York City is nothing like the life you and your girlfriends lived. Except for when it is.

For the past dozen years or so, I have spent months at a time living on my own in New York. Manhattan to be precise. My husband, who was born on the east side of the country, discovered California over three decades ago, about the same time he discovered me, a native-born Californian with the blond hair, hot tub, and two failed marriages to prove it, and decided never to return to his place of birth. Oh, we do attend weddings, anniversaries if they are of a significant number, bat mitzvahs and bar mitzvahs, and big decade birthdays, but as far as Michael is concerned, that is it. I, on the other hand, can't get enough of the densely crowded subways, push and shove of the sea of humans making their way around the island of Manhattan, and everything else one finds in the city. So, I go. And I stay. For weeks and months at a time. And Michael encourages it. He loves me enough to know that if it makes me happy, it makes him happy. Sometimes my friends ask how I get away with leaving for such big chunks of time. Sometimes Michael's buddies ask how they might get their wives to leave them, as long as they leave a freezer filled with turkey lasagna and eggplant casseroles. Even my own father, the leaver of all leavers, wondered about all of this back and forth, back and forth.

It works for us, we tell everyone.

If there is a family event, Michael will arrive and spend a day or two in the city with me before we join in the Sternbach Family Festivities, whatever they may be. I was tucked into my rental on the Upper West Side for a few months when there was just such an event and Michael came to join me.

The streets of Manhattan give him an invisible rash. They make his head pound. He hates to take an elevator to get outside. Lest you think he is totally negative about your city: he isn't. He does love the subway. Something you and your girlfriends didn't seem to make much use of, as I recall. You were all cab girls. But I'm with Michael on this one, I adore the subway. I know it is much complained about and cursed, but until you have lived in a place with no subway, often no sidewalks, and a very limited bus service, you have no idea what a marvel the underground trains are. Even with all of their flaws.

Michael is amazed by the fact that he may fly into
JFK, take the Air-train to the subway in Jamaica,
Queens, get on and ride it into Manhattan, and arrive at
his destination with his bag. Public transportation at a
level we will never know in my part of California. So,
that's what he did. But, Carrie, he arrived frazzled.
Tired. We climbed into bed and turned on the television.
Letterman was on. And outside, it was cold enough to
snow. We had the discussion we always have.

Michael: I do not get what it is you love about this
city. Me: Everything.

Michael: What, do you imagine you are Carrie
Bradshaw, and this is just a giant episode of "Sex and
the City"?

Me: No, not at all!

And that is the truth. I loved watching the show. I
loved all of the characters. But live like you do? Please. I
am old enough that my blond hair is now gray. Yes, I am
a writer, and I do flip open my laptop and sit at a desk and
look out the window, but my subject matter would bore
the knickers off of you and your girlfriends. Although,
make no mistake, I am as passionate about the city as you
are, Carrie.

Back to our being in bed. A king-size bed with
fluffy pillows and a giant cornflower blue comforter.

Me: Let's go for a walk before we go to sleep.
Michael: It's cold.

Me: Yes, it is.

As I am speaking, I am getting out of bed and
pulling on my proper winter coat, purchased in a

second-hand boutique on the Upper East Side, over my flannel, red and white polka dot pajamas. Tucking my feet into my Uggs.

He knows I will be going with him or without. This is one of the aspects of the city I especially love. That at that time of night I feel perfectly safe going for a walk.

He relents.

We are walking on West 85th Street towards Broadway. There are people out grocery shopping, pulling their wheelie carts behind them. There are people walking dogs and taxis are pausing to pick up fares and music is leaking out the door of the Irish pub we pass by. Up ahead is a film crew and their trailers are filling an entire block of Broadway.

This is not an unusual occurrence.

I am almost at the corner when Michael taps me on the shoulder. He has been lagging behind. I turn and he has a strange expression on his face. I look over his shoulder and I am met with a sly smile. Yours, Carrie Bradshaw. Here you were coming up the street right behind Michael. You were wearing a full-skirted pink dress and high heels and we all arrived at the corner at the same time. Someone from the film crew handed you an oversized jacket to put on.

You grinned at my look of surprise. Or my pajamas, I will never know. Me: I love your show?

You: Thank you. Do you want to see Mikhail Baryshnikov? Me. Uh, yes?

You: He is right in front of the McDonald's just down the block! Me: Thank you?

Apparently, when I am a little stunned, I speak only in questions.

After receiving a hug from you, or perhaps you received one from me (let's just call it a draw?), Michael and I took in the sights at the McDonald's, and then toddled back home to bed and discussed how surprised we both were at the famous dancer's diminutive stature.

This is the reason I have chosen to drop you a line, Carrie Bradshaw. In all the years since that night, Michael has never once been able to use the "Sex and the City" line on me again. Because you never know when you will find yourself actually living in Carrie Bradshaw's neighborhood. I thank you for that?

With love and affection,
Claudia

Carrie Bradshaw isn't real. She appeared first in a book, Sex and the City, *written by Candace Bushnell and, when the book was turned into an HBO series, Sarah Jessica Parker played Carrie.*

Carrie, who, as I said does not exist, is a writer and lover of fashion. She, again as I have said, rarely, if ever, used public transportation, despite living off the wages of a newspaper columnist. After the series ended, two Sex and the City *films were released. I give super points to my husband, Michael, for sitting through the first one without complaint.*

Dear Edie Falco and Stanley Tucci,

Well, that was unexpected. I mean all of the bare ass scenes on the revival of Terrence McNally's "Frankie & Johnny at the Clair de Lune". I will say, you each have excellent asses, and I can say that honestly, as my husband Michael and I were seated in the second row of the New York theater.

I wasn't sure if the three older women in front of us were more shocked, or perhaps thrilled, at all of the sex scenes. They tittered loudly (can a titter be loud?), at times. Especially when you, Stanley, bounced up and down on the bed in your birthday suit. It was great theater. And the night had started out on a high note. As high as Stanley could jump!

First, there had been a romantic dinner with wine and candles at one of my favorite French bistros on the Upper West Side, followed by a stroll down to midtown to the theater. We held hands. We needed an evening like this. There had been very little going on in the romance department at our house. And it was my fault.

I mean, if there was blame to be assigned, I was the one who should step up and accept it. Okay, maybe not me, as in I was being stubborn or cold or refusing Michael's attention just to be cruel, but it was my body causing the chill between us physically.

Fucking breast cancer. Fucking hysterectomy. Fucking no hormones.

I was "over it," but cancer casts a long shadow, and we were still in the dark when it came to our sex lives. Surgeries, organs removed, which once upon a time had aided in having a healthy physical relationship with my husband. Treatment, medications, etc. All had taken their toll. And, while some women fall in love and marry older men who may or may not have been bothered by this whole new world, depending on their supply of blue pills, I had, years ago, fallen in love with a man eight years younger who still had the vigor of an 18-year-old. And until now, the difference in age seemed unimportant.

Well, fuck me.

I was so engrossed in the play and the bouncing and the three women in front of us that I failed to notice how quiet Michael had become. At intermission, I ducked into the ladies' room, while Michael went to the bar. We both made it back to our seats at the same time and the lights quickly dimmed once again.

I was, in reality and as a metaphor, in the dark when it came to my husband's mood. Oh Edie, Stanley, you two were so good. The sex scenes so real, I felt like a peeping Tom. The acting was superb. And because I was still feeling the thrill of not dying from cancer (even though I never thought I actually would), I just blocked out any negative feelings about life, or the night, or anything else. I was on a high. But let me say, that can be a little bit self-centered. I was focused on me. ME. I was changed, for sure. And I wasn't as sensitive as I might have been when it came to my sweet, kind, hardworking, loving, sex-starved husband.

You received a standing ovation at the end of the play. But while I stood there clapping like a trained seal, I noticed Michael easing his way to the end of the row. As I caught up with him, he slipped on his jacket and walked out of the theater, his hands stuffed into his pockets. He didn't look back to see if I was following. He just walked at a fast pace, something he rarely does. Usually when we are in New York City, I am the one waiting for him to catch up.

But with my theater buzz at full throttle, I trotted towards him and attempted to link my arm through his. He shook me off, then looked me in the face. I hardly recognized him. The anger, not at me, but at the situation, was plain to see. The pain in his eyes evident. Because here is the thing: while my body was incapable of performing at the level it once had, his was fully functioning. And when one's body shuts down, at least in my case, the brain accepts it. I missed our old sex life if I thought about it, but I was becoming used to not thinking about it. And I had dragged Michael to a live theater experience which was filled with SEX. My poor husband sat and watched two people actually do what we couldn't (okay, maybe, just maybe, they didn't actually do the deed, but it sure looked real from the second row), for two hours.

Clearly, I had not thought this through when I purchased the tickets. Again, fuck me. Or actually don't. Because I can't.

I wish there had been a full moon, so I could end this letter telling you how we strolled in the park in the heavenly glow and kissed in the shadows knowing all would be well in our world. But there wasn't. Michael continued up the street at a pace beyond my capabilities. I kept my eye on him so he wouldn't get lost. I know the city. He is not as familiar. And while walking, I realized I had a lot to learn about this new territory in which we were now living. I wasn't the only one who had had to deal with cancer and its aftermath. Michael was right there in the trenches with me. And he had been since the diagnosis. He had been amazing. Supportive, devoted, caring. And he got fucked by it too.

I finally caught up to him. And the rest of the evening was strained. There were tears; I won't say whose. And, finally, we had the conversation, which I suppose had been waiting to be had for quite some time.

We began to rebuild what had been burned down. As time passed, we finally turned a corner and could see a future, changed, but still rich with possibilities. You, Edie and Stanley, triggered the conversation. Pleasant, easy? Not at all. But I thank you both.

With gratitude,
Claudia

P.S. So, did you, or didn't you?

Edie Falco was born in 1963. She may be best known for playing Carmela Soprano, the mob wife of Tony Soprano in the HBO show, The Sopranos. *You would not want to fuck with her. She also played the title character in Showtime's* Nurse Jackie. *Again, don't cross her.*

She seems to always be working.

If you can catch her on stage (live theater is lucky to have such a talented, gritty, afraid of nothing actor), grab a ticket.

Stanley Tucci was born in 1960. Today I suspect that he is known by the younger generation as Caesar Flickerman in the film franchise, The Hunger Games. *I especially enjoyed him in* The Devil Wears Prada *where he is not a bad guy, just a rather put-upon employee in a tough business: fashion. He has had a prolific career in films as well as on stage.*

And he looks pretty, pretty good stark naked.

Dear Andrea Bocelli,

First, let me say how appalled I was when, a few years ago, I read a review in a major newspaper and realized the author of the article was actually quite unfamiliar with your work. She apparently didn't even spend a minute or two learning anything about you. She criticized your performing style. Said something about "singing with your eyes closed" all of the time. Upon reading that slam, I wanted to shake her by her shoulders and ask her how she earned her reporter's credentials.

Knowing, as everyone else who knows anything about you does, that you are blind, I hoped that perhaps you never actually heard her uninformed opinion about your work. But I am guessing one of your people clued you in. As a former columnist and feature writer for another paper, I apologize on behalf of journalists everywhere. I don't know what ever happened to her, but her editor also deserves a bit of a smack down. I do hope that they each learned from their blunder. Seriously, bad form on their part. This is not why I am writing to you today though. But as long as I was at my desk and striking up this one-way conversation, why not try to correct a wrong even though it is years after the fact.

I am writing this morning while listening to you sing. For the past few years, I have avoided your music. I've missed your soaring, emotional tenor. But, Andrea, I can now listen and feel something deeper than the simple joy I once felt. Feelings much more complex. Joy, grief, wonder, gratitude. Thus, the thank-you note.

When my sister Carol called me from her car one fall day to tell me she was getting married, I also experienced a storm of emotions. It had only been a few days earlier that she called to tell me she was dying. But, before she departed this life, she and her partner of more than two decades were going to invite a handful of close friends, and then, in front of us all, promise to love each other until death would part them. Would I write something for it? she asked. Of course, I told her. I then hung up and sat at my kitchen table until the sun began to set and Michael's pickup pulled into the driveway.

Hours had passed. I met him on the front walkway and let him comfort me just as he had promised to do when we married more than 30 years ago.

As I write this, I am again at my kitchen table. But it is morning and there is a full pot of coffee keeping me company. And your voice.

I imagined that writing something for the wedding was going to be difficult, but surprisingly, it wasn't. Your music inspired me. Your passion fueled me. And when, one week later, we gathered at my sister's house, it was you who supplied the music for the evening. We were all in our finest. My sister Carol waited at the top of the stairs and as you sang "The Prayer", she slowly descended and joined her future wife in front of the fireplace. There were flowers everywhere. And a beautiful wedding cake. And tears as I watched her commit to her partner for a lifetime. We all knew her lifetime was quickly coming to an end. That she would be leaving her wife, her twin, Cheryl, and me, the eldest sister. Oh Carol, how could this be? Oh, Andrea, thank you for your voice. What you brought to that evening.

After the ceremony, before the cake was cut, Carol and her new bride were toasted by many. I was the last at bat. My hand shook as I read out loud what I hoped would be appropriate for the occasion. I could not meet Carol's eyes. It would have been the end of any emotional control.

"Be fully present in this moment. Feel your breath rise and fall. What came before is over and to try to see ahead will blind you to all that is happening in this room as you stand here surrounded by love.

Be mindful of the small details in every moment. The clock ticking and the trill of a song bird and the wind as it rattles each leaf on the tree. Notice the light as it shifts and shimmers. Step outside after the sun has slipped into the Pacific and contemplate the night sky. Sit silently and try to imagine space and beyond. Let it take your breath away.

Give it your full attention. A minute fully experienced can seem like a lifetime. A gift often unnoticed.

Tonight, I wish you millions of moments. Each one so exquisite they are impossible to describe. Each one as lustrous as a newly formed pearl. Collect them. String them together on golden threads and wear them forever."

Then I cut the cake.

It was a lovely evening. And a few weeks later, we had a lovely funeral. You were there as well. And as I sat alone, still stunned by all that had taken place, I listened to you as you sang.

"Lead us to a place, guide us with your grace, to a place where we'll be safe."

I tend to believe there is no place where we will be safe. But thanks to you, my sister believed there might be. Your songs gave her comfort. And for that I am immeasurably grateful.

Now, more than four years after the events, I find I can listen to you once again. And when I do, I always, always think of Carol.

With deep gratitude,
Claudia

Andrea Bocelli was born in Italy in 1958. Sighted at birth, he became completely blind at the age of 12 after a football accident. He travels the world performing to sold out audiences everywhere.

Michael took me to one last year, and OMG he was good.

The record producer, David Foster (who, small world that it is, was married to a Real Housewife of Beverly Hills!), has stated that Mr. Bocelli has the most beautiful voice in the world.

I would not argue.

Dear Carol,

It was the last time I saw you alive. It was after all had transpired, all the terrible things said. I had been given the opportunity to see you once more for 30 minutes. Michael drove, as my state of mind was still fragile.

Your wife had absented herself at my request. I couldn't risk having her there. Her knives were too sharp.

Michael asked Cheryl to leave us alone. I could no longer lie next to you in bed; you were in too much pain. Just the movement of the mattress made you cringe. I sat quietly with you and things were said between us. Words I will keep for myself. I will place them in a silver locket and wear them around my neck until I die. I will read them again and again. They will comfort me, I hope, in the days to come. I said nothing about what had transpired between your wife and myself. The last thing I wanted to do was cause you pain or add to your suffering.

Then my time was almost up.

I was on my knees at the side of your bed. My face inches from yours. My beloved. "What," I begged, "can I do for you? Anything."

"Make up with my wife," you asked. "I will," I promised.

"And don't say goodbye," you whispered.

"See you later," I said and kissed your forehead. Your cheek. My tears mixing with yours.

Michael and Cheryl came back up the stairs and were waiting in the hall. I was blinded by my tears. Michael lead me downstairs and out into the bright, scalding, sunlight.

I climbed in the car and Michael patted me on the leg. We drove to the end of the block to make a U-turn and, when we got to your house, your wife was standing out front. She had just returned home.

Stop, I told Michael. And before I could explain what I was about to do, to myself or to him, I jumped out of the car and grabbed her firmly by the arm. I lead her back into the cool, darkness of the house and up the hardwood stairs. I was noisy, wanting to make sure that you would be awake when we entered your room.

You were so still I was afraid you had left us already.

"Carol," I called out. You opened your eyes and your surprise was evident. I looked deeply into your blue eyes as I wrapped my arms around your wife and said to her, "I love you. I love you. I love you."

Because I would do anything for you. Even deceive you.

Carol, your face relaxed. Tears kept flowing but there was peace in the room.

All the way home, I thought about how lucky I was to be able to grant your dying wish, while carrying the guilt of having told a complete and total lie.

Forever grateful,
Claude

Dear Carol,

I miss you. Your funeral was well-attended. Even the members of your old softball team showed up. All in their 60s now, I didn't recognize them. But they knew me! And they were so happy to see Cheryl.

I need to confess. I may have made a tiddle bit of a scene. I am hoping it went unnoticed. Before the funeral at the church, we were to meet at the funeral home (by the way, that is a creepy thing to call a place like that "home"?).

There were multiple rooms, and some of us were gathered in the lobby of the "home." A kind-looking gentleman directed us to another room, inviting us to visit you.

Let me just say here, I was not at my best that day.

We left the lobby area and entered an area where I believe others were sitting, however, I really didn't notice them. I only saw you at the front of the room, resting in a casket. The lid was up. You were wearing your pretty black and white dress. The one with the short sleeve black jacket. Your wedding dress.

Your hair was done. Your makeup perfect, although I would have forgone the artificial eyelashes. I never saw you wear them in life, so why now?

Anyway, I don't know what I was expecting to see in that room, but if I had thought I was going to find you, really you, I was greatly disappointed and may have made my feelings known.

I did go up and say hello, goodbye. Then just turned to Michael, buried my wet face in his chest and may have said in a voice others might have heard, "She's not here."

Then I believe I made a quick, perhaps undignified, exit.

I may have made a small, emotional ruckus.

I offer no excuse other than my heart was hurting to the point I thought actual breakage was eminent.

That isn't all.

After the service, after Michael and the other pallbearers carried you out of the church and into the overly bright sunshine, you were placed into the back of the hearse. The back doors were left open. People gathered in the bright sunlight to cry and chat on the steps. Then there was movement which led me to believe someone was going to shut the door and drive away with you. I felt the panic rising in my chest and pushed my way through the crowd. I was afraid I might actually climb in the back of the vehicle and refuse to let you go.

I made it to the back doors and placed my hands on the casket as if that would stop everything. Undo what had been done. It was December, but so warm I could feel the sweat dripping down my back, soaking my black dress.

Michael pulled me away. It may have been a small scene. I don't know. Perhaps no one noticed at all.

I hope I didn't embarrass you. I hope if you knew it was happening you understood. Did you know that my love was/is so strong? Do you feel the same?

In any case, because I never said it enough, thank you for being such a brilliant, brave, strong, intelligent, loving sister. The empty space at the table will never be filled.

In love and sorrow,
Claude

Dear Mrs. Day,

In 1955, you began to teach me to read. In a class filled with kindergartners of various learning abilities, you had a way of knowing exactly which student would be interested in what. At least that is what I recall. And once you had helped me crack the code, I gobbled up books like I was an addict and they were crack. I have never been able to quit!

I wonder how many of your students developed the same addiction. I wonder how many got to spend most of their careers reading and writing their way through decades of growing up, growing old.

I am now retired. A couple of years ago, the literary journal I edited officially discontinued. We ran out of funding. It happens. I loved my job. I was paid to read the work of other writers all day long. Paid to read! To be fair, some of it was horrible. But, oh, when I would discover a gem. The feeling was similar, I am sure, to seeing the shimmer of gold in the pan of silt and muck.

I wonder if you felt a similar feeling when you discovered an especially gifted student? Oh, I do hope so.

If, when I was a child with my nose in a book, someone would have told me that a job reading often great writing existed, and that I would someday have it, I would have willingly believed in just about anything one might have told me.

Unicorns. The tooth fairy. Fathers returning home. Singing frogs with iridescent wings.

Reading saved me when I was young. My sisters had each other. Twins in their own bubble. Their own universe. They loved the same things. Spoke the same language. I did not feel alone. But I felt singular to their double. Aware that I stood outside their sphere. It was a plain and simple fact.

My mother never asked me where Carol was. Or where Cheryl was. She would ask, where are the twins? She never asked me to watch one or the other. Keep an eye on the girls, she would say.

I didn't always obey. I retreated to whatever book I was in love with at the time. "The Borrowers", "The Boxcar Children", "The Bobbsey Twins", or "Henry Huggins". And thanks to you, Mrs. Day, I could get lost in between the covers.

The twins? I don't know where they were. I didn't care! I was setting up house in an abandoned boxcar with a completely different set of siblings.

Our elementary school library was in a portable just down the hill from our school, and you would issue me a pass once my work was complete, and I could cut across the playground, walk down the narrow path between rows of ice plants, and enter the library.

I could say I recall golden shafts of light pouring through the high windows. But that may be attaching more romance to the place than it actually warrants. I do remember the librarian. Not her name, but a detail so personal that I am still surprised I know it. She was rather short. She had hair like Mamie Eisenhower. She wore flower print dresses which dipped open at the neck when she bent over her desk or knelt down to reach a book on a low shelf. She was missing a breast. In its place was a pale pink pad tucked into her bra. It looked like a large powder puff. Maybe she smelled like talcum powder or maybe that is simply what I imagined the first time I glimpsed her secret. I was not shocked by it. My grandmother wore the same accessory. I don't recall if I knew what this very personal detail of a woman's missing anatomy meant, but I would learn eventually. I did know it was not to be spoken about.

I don't recall if the librarian was especially kind or not. She may have enjoyed my enthusiastic search for books to devour, or she may have never even noticed how much time I spent in her kingdom. But I loved it all. The ritual of checking out a book.

Taking the card out of the envelope glued to the inside of the cover. Seeing the names of those who had read it before me. Sometimes seeing my own name if I was returning to a book I considered an old friend.

Watching as the librarian placed the metal stamp over the pocket and pressed down. The new due date now added to the list. The smell of purple ink. There was a three- book limit. No matter. I knew I could get three more as soon as I had finished the three in hand.

Books saved me.

Books are saving me once again.

Every night, Michael and I climb in to bed at the same time. We turn on our bedside lights and rest our books against our knees and read. At some point Michael turns to me and says, "I'm about done."

I ask, "Ten more minutes?" "Okay."

(I wonder how often you had to ask me to put away a book so I could learn my numbers. I wonder if I begged for just a smidgen more time?)

Then the lights go out and he drops off quickly. I do not. My mind begins to fill with thoughts I don't want. Images. Voices. I try to meditate. I count backwards.

One hundred ripe apricots.

Ninety-nine ripe apricots, 98, 97, and on and on.

Michael has always advised me to "go to my happy place" when trying to fall asleep. I have a few of them. But one is the house my father lived in when I was a teenager. I didn't visit often, but I remember being there in the summer for a weekend. He had horses and a long winding driveway lined with apricot trees. I recall a Sunday morning being sent down to the bottom of the hill to fetch the newspaper. I plucked ripe apricots from the trees as I walked in the August heat. Horses came running as I stood on the middle slat of the wooden fence picking sun-warmed fruit from the trees. Their noses were as smooth as velvet as they nudged me, sniffing and whinnying.

I could not believe that this was how some people lived, let alone my own father. Horses, apricots for the picking, a Spanish-style house on the top of the hill overlooking everything. Balconies! There were even strutting peacocks. (Only later would I see the obviousness of my father keeping such vane, showy birds.) I was happy that morning. I wanted to stop time. So, sometimes it is where I go when I try to count myself to sleep. I picture walking in an orchard and filling my basket with extravagantly juicy fruit. The hum and drone of bees above me. Then eating each apricot as I continue on my way.

So, I count. One hundred down to 0. My basket empty, I reverse the process and begin at the number one.

Fuck. This night I have emptied and filled my basket again and again and I am still awake. I head to the big blue sofa in the living room. The Ikea couch. It is so comfortable that, when we first bought it, brought it home in pieces and then built it, relishing its size, its L shape, I never wanted to leave it. Even though they had given us the wrong slip covers.

So, it sat bare while we waited for new ones. I didn't care. There was the sofa in all its glory, looking like a blindingly white collection of giant sanitary napkins.

"Really?" Michael asked as I reclined on it, book in hand.

"We could bring the old couch back in and take this apart until the covers get here," he suggested.

No. I had found my bliss. Covered or not. It was plush, big, and I imagine super absorbent. It wasn't going anywhere.

Eventually the slipcovers arrived. Perfection was achieved.

It is the middle of the night. I leave our bed and head towards the couch. I turn on the small lamp on the table behind it and suddenly it is an island retreat. At first, I used a woven shawl as a throw to keep me warm while I read. Soon I decided it wasn't adequate. Not large enough to suit my needs. So, one afternoon I drove down to our village. Yes, we have a village. I went to the charming shop where I purchased the throw for my sister and her wife months earlier as a wedding gift. I chose a blanket woven with purples and reds and oranges and blues. It is delicious. It is a luxury.

I read an entire book a night sometimes. If it is thick, it will last two nights.

I have lost myself in "The Goldfinch" by Donna Tart, "The Interestings" by Meg Wolitzer, "The Luminaries" (3 nights!) by Eleanor Catton. I sink into "All the Light We Cannot See" by Anthony Doerr, "Life After Life" by Kate Atkinson, "The Signature of All Things" by Elizabeth Gilbert and David Gilbert's exquisite novel, "& Sons".

I watch as stacks of books grow, sprouting like mushrooms all over the house. I cannot get enough. I am insatiable.

But, Mrs. Day, where is the book that will tell me who I am now? I am not the eldest sister, loved by the younger twins. I may never have been that person. I thought I was.

Up is down. Left is right. Pluto is no longer a planet. I am no longer the beloved big sister. Oh, I know that I will always be Cheryl's older sibling. And I was Carol's eldest sibling. But sister and all that that implies?

Perhaps not. Perhaps not. I just had no idea.

Did anyone ever ask Pluto how she felt about her demotion?

Perhaps Pluto, being very sure of what she is, simply said, "Fuck it. What do they know? Mere mortals."

I continue to read. The hands on the clock go round and round. The house is quiet. Michael is sleeping. Down in Los Angeles, my daughter is sleeping. In her belly, the baby boy is sleeping. Somewhere in Europe, where he is making a movie, the boy's father is sleeping.

I am the only person in the world awake. Here on my island. Here in my tent. Safe.

I wish I could tell you how much I appreciate the time you spent teaching me how to read. I had no idea it would be part of my salvation.

Did you?

Respectfully,
Claudia

P.S. Remember when you busted me for sucking my thumb in class? My face is still red!

Dear Tim Gunn,

When I was in high school, I used to make my mother dresses for her to wear to work. Although I take pride in that fact, I also know that not one of them would have brought me success on your show, "Project Runway".

My mother didn't sew. I took a sewing class in school which was part of the Home Ec program. To help prepare me for life in the real world, I learned how to make a tangy vinaigrette, potato leek soup, and chocolate pudding from scratch. I also learned how to make a dirndl skirt (I made it in black cotton with white rickrack around the bottom!) and how to put in a zipper. Our instructor was determined to teach us how to make facings and pleats of equal size. Also, how to make pockets and bound buttonholes. I failed bound buttonholes. But it didn't stop me. I simply used buttons for decoration and hidden snaps to hold things together.

My friend Susie Peterson's mother did know how to sew. She gave me tips once I had completed the class, and I was such a motivated designer I got a small, used Singer sewing machine. A little black marvel with gold detailing.

Nothing gave me more pleasure than going to the fabric store and wandering up and down the aisles with the of bolts of fabric, imagining what I might make. It was the sixties, so a yard of fabric could be turned into a sleeveless mini dress in no time. A yard and a quarter would mean I could add pockets. But for my mother's dresses, a full two yards were required. Taking the bus home from downtown Oakland with a large bag filled to the brim with material of all colors and patterns was bliss.

I had one dress pattern for my mother. It was a simple A-line design. I could, using that simple shape, add a collar or attach a belt at the back with the aforementioned decorative buttons. I could make it sleeveless or add sleeves. It could have pockets, inset or patch, it could be a floral print, solid color, striped, or checked. Striped or checked did require a bit more fabric so the lines or squares might be matched up. I remember a lime green number and a wild orange and yellow. They took very little time to construct once I had a good handle on how the pattern was to be laid out and cut and put together.

After school, while my younger twin sisters were out playing softball on the corner or riding skateboards down our hill with the boys in the neighborhood, I would settle in at the kitchen table with my black machine and get cranking.

I was careful. I steam ironed every seam and every facing. I watched the clock, knowing my mother would pull into our driveway by 6 p.m.

My goal was to have the finished piece ironed and hung on the laundry room door by the time she got home from a long day at the cookie factory where she was in charge of balancing the books.

I loved the whole process. The feel of crisp cotton as I cut the pattern out. The smell of the steam as I ironed. How quickly the fabric would go from wrinkled to smooth. The pride I felt when I would, at last, hang it up for my mother to see. And she wore them! She wore them with excitement! She was as proud as I was.

She was a single mother when that was quite unusual. She was tired most of the time, and now, as I am in my sixties and I think about all she accomplished, keeping us all fed, clothed, out of trouble, I think of how remarkable she was. And brave. Brave enough to wear my dresses to work. They must have looked like a school project, mustn't they?

Once I left home, my sewing slowed to a stop. Moving around from city to city, apartment to apartment, eventually I lost track of my little Singer. I didn't take up the needle and thread again until I was a mother and made tiny little cotton dresses for my daughter. Then she hit an age where leggings and t-shirts were her favorite modes of dress, putting me out of business.

But I never forgot the feeling of accomplishment I derived from taking a piece of cotton or wool or once even, silk, and creating something that no one else had.

Not long ago, I lost one of my sisters to cancer. No matter what I did, or how hard I tried, I was having a terrible time getting over it. Moving forward. I was wrapped in sadness. I wore my grief like a heavy blanket wrapped around my shoulders. I began to watch more television than usual. And I discovered "Project Runway".

Every week, I would tune in to see what the challenge was. How the contestants would do. I loved the runway show at the end of each episode. I didn't really care who won; I just wanted to see what they had created.

Light bulb moment!

I went online and ordered a new sewing machine. I went to the fabric store and spent hours trying to decide what to make. What to make it out of. The possibilities were endless. I had forgotten how it felt to have endless possibilities.

I continued to watch "Project Runway", and sometimes had my machine set up and my newest project laid out while watching. My first, a used, full-length chocolate brown cashmere coat which was lush, but exceedingly large on me, was a bit more complicated than I was ready for. Taking apart, cutting down, and then rebuilding was quite a challenge. But I didn't really mind. I felt too happy and grateful that I had rediscovered my long-ago passion. When I had finished the remodel and tried it on, I had to admit it was a bit of a mess. A disaster actually. But I didn't really care. I kept at it.

My sewing skills have not improved much. Nothing I make would qualify me for a spot on "Project Runway". But that doesn't matter a lick.

A few months ago, I was in New York. I try to never miss the exhibit at the Costume Institute at the Metropolitan Museum. Every year, something new and different is on display. This latest exhibit was focused on the clothing designed by a talented Japanese artist. Pieces had sleeves where no sleeves were needed. Arm holes sewn shut. Lumpy shoulder pads and all manner of strange detailing. I couldn't imagine my high school sewing teacher giving the designer a passing grade. But they were fantastic. I didn't care about how one would wear them. They just made me happy looking at them. And, actually, my reworked cashmere coat would have fit in beautifully!

Leaving the museum, I decided to walk through Central Park to the west side to pick up some fresh-squeezed grapefruit juice at my favorite market. Tequila was waiting for me at home and the combo makes for a most satisfying summer (fall, winter, spring) cocktail.

There is a small tunnel, which leads to the Great Lawn, behind the museum. It is called Greywacke Arch. Usually there is a musician playing an instrument just inside. I keep a dollar or two in my pocket to encourage his playing.

As I walked closer to the tunnel, the shape of a gentleman could be seen exiting the shadowed space. As he stepped out into the sunlight and continued in my direction, I realized who it was. It was you, Mr. Gunn!

You were dressed nattily. Your light blue shirt crisp. Your lavender tie knotted beautifully. Cuffs, linked, peeked out from the sleeves of your elegant bespoke suit. And of course, a perfectly folded pocket square.

Speak or don't speak, becomes the question when an opportunity such as this presents itself.

I spoke. I thanked you for your show and told you I had just taken up sewing again. You held my hand, patting it while you did so, and thanked me for thanking you. All the while

I was fully aware of what I was wearing and quite disappointed in my wardrobe choice. What was I doing wandering around in a city where one could run into Tim Gunn, dressed in jeans and a t-shirt? And, sin of all sins, flip-flops! I promised myself I would do better. Although for this particular encounter, it was obviously too late. It was over in seconds. You went on your way. I went on mine.

Later, back at the apartment, cocktail in hand, I sat at the dining room table looking out at the upper east side and began to think about what I might make next. I wasn't thinking about how much I missed my sister. I wasn't reliving having to tell my mother she had passed. I wasn't revisiting the funeral. I was only thinking about sewing and creating and remembering those days when I could hear my sisters outside playing with all the boys in the neighborhood, laughing, cheering, arguing, running inside at the end of the day sweaty and noisy while I sat at the kitchen table using every bit of my imagination and my limited skills, making something I hoped my mother would love.

Thank you, Mr. Gunn, for helping me reach that point.

Respectfully yours,
Claudia

Tim Gunn was born in 1953. He is a snappy dresser and hosts the reality show, Project Runway. *He served on the faculty of Parsons School of Design at the New School in New York City from 1982 until 2007. He knows his stuff. (I was going to say shit, but I don't believe Mr. Gunn would use that phrase.)*

He seems to be a sweet, kind and thoughtful man. However, I really am projecting here. He is known for the phrase "make it work," which I believe is a good philosophy to carry through life.

Mr. Gunn has left Project Runaway *for other adventures. He is missed.*

Dear Carol,

You have been gone almost four months. Michael has taken me to Kauai. Or I have taken him. A few weeks ago, I logged on to Airbnb and found a nest that looked promising. Breakfast would be delivered to our door each day. Beaches were in walking distance. A small town was listed as just a short drive from our bungalow. It all looked heavenly.

Oh, Carol. We spent one week on the lush, tropical island. We drove a rented Mustang convertible, top down, on the narrow highway up and down the coast. We kayaked on a river, swam and snorkeled in the warm, calm waters. We hiked to the Queen's Bath and dove in the clear pool created by nature. We ate and drank and I watched myself from the opposite shore as I tried to feel what was happening. Tried to experience the perfection that was all around. But it was as if I was looking at elegant pastries in a bakery window, hands on the glass, face pressed against the smooth surface. I could imagine, but I was unable to smell or taste or savor the rich delicacies right in front of me. And in truth, I had no appetite at all.

One evening, while in a bar and drinking tequila, we listened to three local musicians playing slack-key guitar. They asked where folks were from. A gentleman called out, Santa Cruz. What a small world, I thought. Our own home town!

A few minutes later, he and his wife were passing by, and Michael placed his hand on the husband's arm.

"Did you say Santa Cruz?" Michael asked.

"Yes," said the tanned, gray-haired man. He then explained that years ago they fell in love with Kauai, the people, the food and music, and bought a place. They now spend months at a time in the tropics.

I wonder, if you had lived, if you might have done something similar. Purchased a slice of Paradise for you and your wife. I wonder so many things about what you would have done, if you had had a future.

Michael then introduced himself to the couple and added, "This is my wife, Claudia." He explained that we too lived in the California beach town.

The husband looked at me and asked with surprise, "Claudia Sternbach? Are you Claudia Sternbach? From the newspaper?"

"I am," I confessed, and wondered at the size of the world and the connections we share, often not even knowing. A random gentleman in a Hawaiian print shirt, thousands of miles away from home, compliments me on my career as a newspaper columnist. He has reminded me that I existed before that horrible evening in your bedroom. I still do. Perhaps this feeling of being a shadow, as insubstantial as mist, is temporary. I have been recognized as a solid, three-dimensional person. By a stranger.

On our last night on the island, I began to cough. Vog, we were told, was a problem. A kind of fog, smog, funk in the air caused by volcanic ash. Have you ever heard of that? Seriously, trouble in paradise!

I didn't know it at the time, but it would linger for weeks. It was made worse by high winds at home. Winds carrying small particles, which would make friends with the ash already in my lungs.

I drank copious amounts of hot tea with honey and lemon. I visited the doctor, who advised me to stay out of the wind. To be patient. To take medicine to weaken the cough. To keep as silent as possible.

I had dreams of you and Cheryl. In one dream, we were taking boxes of Jell-O from the kitchen cabinet, something we used to do as kids. I dreamt I was sitting on the floral print couch in our old living room with the blue carpet. I tore the corner off the top of the box of Jell-O, licked my finger and dipped it in. Sucking on my finger, I was thrilled by the sweet, tart flavor. I dipped again and again, my finger turning cherry red. I continued until I put my finger in my mouth and found the taste had changed. It was dry and chalky. My finger was coated with gray. Looking into the box, I noticed the Jell-O was gone, replaced by ashes.

In my dream, I was now an adult, alone on the couch in my childhood home. I was holding your remains in the palm of my hand.

Love,
Claude

Dear Jonathan Franzen,

This is not my first thank you note to you. However, each time in the past that I have tried to express my gratitude, you tell me that it is you, not I, who should be grateful. Really? I mean I was the person on the receiving end of free housing in New York City for summer after summer after summer. And sometimes winter, spring, and fall. A gift I still have trouble processing.

Yes, I did forward your mail to you in California. Yes, I sent you a pair of dress pants I found hanging in your closet when you had a wedding to attend and didn't want to purchase new pants when you knew there was a perfectly fine pair on the Upper East Side of Manhattan. Yes, there was that time you requested I send you a small tube of something medicinal, which had been residing in your sock drawer. But still.

Over the past several years or so, I would definitely say that you, my dear friend, have improved the quality of my life much more than I have added to yours. But, confession, when meeting you for the first time, I did have a small chip on my shoulder. Because of you, I was in danger of losing one of my best girlfriends and writing buddies to you and to New York City.

It was at my Friday night writing group in Santa Cruz, California, that I first heard your name. My friend Kathy mentioned you. She seemed a bit smitten. You lived in a city 3,000 miles away from our coastal community. She began making trips to see you. The handwriting was on the wall. This was serious. She was taken by your writing. She was impressed with your dedication to your work. I had not yet read any of your novels. "The Corrections" had yet to be born, so, even though you had a strong publishing history, you hadn't yet become a household name. But Kathy recognized your talent immediately, which I knew to be high praise indeed, because Kathy is herself a brilliant writer.

Anyway, Jon, I remember the first time we met. I happened to be in New York for a few weeks and Kathy was in town visiting you. She suggested we all meet for a drink at a corner cafe on the Upper West Side. We did.

My first impression was that you were tall. I believe you had come from your workspace up in Harlem. I seem to remember that each of us had traveled from different spots on the island. Kathy had come from across town, you from uptown and I from the far West Side.

As we sat on small bistro chairs in the summer sun, enjoying cocktails and the passing shoppers, diners and office workers heading home, you asked me about my writing. I was so relieved to be able to say that I had, in fact, had a book published and was working on another. Kathy too had had a book published and you were doing the final rewrites on "The Corrections".

We were equals! I contemplated giving you some advice on what to expect when your book came out. Yes, I wanted to tell you. It is rather exciting to see your name on the cover. Yes, it is rather rewarding to attend your high school reunion and be able to say, "I'm a writer." And then be able to back it up with proof ... a real memoir published by a real publishing house. But, I wanted to warn you, don't expect it to change your life.

Dozens of people bought my book and my life was unchanged. I didn't want you to have high expectations when it came to your book and the reception it might receive.

I'm so glad I kept my mouth shut.

"The Corrections" made a substantial splash in the literary pond. More like a tidal wave. And it not only changed your life; it changed mine.

You had been living in an adorable one-bedroom apartment on Lexington Ave. It even had a window which looked out onto a tree, if I recall. But now you were free to live a little larger. You began to look for a new place and, one evening, you joined Kathy and me at a French restaurant looking like a kid on Christmas morning. You had made an offer on an apartment in a building you had long admired and it looked as if you had been approved. You were thrilled and I was excited for you.

I did not anticipate that your new digs would become my summer home while you and Kathy spent months at a time in California. That I would give up my temporary rental on the Upper West Side and become an Upper East Sider. And that for years, I would sleep in your bed, write at your desk, hang my clothes in your closet, and entertain my friends at your dining room table. And yet, that is exactly what happened.

Jon, because of you I developed relationships with doormen! I made friends with the residents of the building! I got to sit at the kitchen window and watch the first snowfall of the season while sipping tequila, feather-like flakes drifting past.

There were the years my daughter was living in the city and she and her friends would stop by. All actors, I would get to go see them in their Off-Broadway plays. And later, when she was married, and both she and her husband lived in the city along with their new baby, I was close enough to be able to babysit. To keep him overnight and actually sleep next to a small, borrowed cradle which housed my Darling Boy.

Because of you, I was able to tuck my grandson into a stroller, Dr. Seuss quilt wrapped around him, and walk through Central Park to the boat pond, and then to the Alice in Wonderland statue always covered in climbing children.

I was able to join the Metropolitan Museum and spend hours every week furthering my education. I enjoyed concerts at Carnegie Hall and events at Lincoln Center. New York City became not my second home, but in my heart, my first.

I did go on to finish a second book and one of the highlights of my life was you introducing me at a book store on the Upper East side and I became, in my mind at least, a real New York Writer!

We won't worry about how small the crowd was. It still counts!

The apartment also became my retreat. When my sister died, and I could not find any peace, I hid there. I found that if your heart is broken, it is still broken, no matter how far you travel or how long you hide, but it was such a comfort to be able to wrap myself in sorrow there in that space. To know that I could stay in bed for days if I felt like it and that, with a quick phone call, warm food would be delivered, and a bottle of wine could be ordered, and that a reliable man at the door would buzz me to let me know that my needs were about to be met.

Oh, how I thank you for giving me that.

You have sold the apartment now and become a full-time resident of California. But, sometimes Jon, when I can't sleep at night, I go to the apartment in my mind. I remember the absolute thrill of walking out the front door of the building and having the entire city at my disposal. The freedom to do whatever I felt like. To head north or south, east or west. To stroll along a river or subway down to one of the Villages.

You gave me the city, Jon.

Forever in your debt,
Claudia xo

Jonathan Franzen was born in 1959 in Western Springs, Illinois to parents who I am guessing could not have imagined the success he would have. He is a novelist, and essayist, and once had his face on the cover of Time magazine where it was stated that he was a "Great American Novelist".

I concur.

After living in New York City for decades, he now resides in Santa Cruz, California where he watches birds. When there aren't enough birds for him in his own backyard, he travels the globe looking for more.

Then he writes about it.

He is kind and smart and generous, obviously. I loved sleeping in his bed.

Dear Jane,

I am attempting to honor your privacy, so no last name, but still want to thank you publicly. If not for you, I would never have had the opportunity to ride in the back seat of a car worth more than my house, headed out for a sumptuous Italian dinner while cuddling with a cloned dog.

I have asked around and, so far, no one else I have queried has confessed to having such an experience.

You and I had a history going back long enough that I knew and was quite fond of the original dog from which not one, but two dogs were duplicated. Oh, she was a sweet- natured canine. And the only time I was in the car with her, she was extremely mellow. Although it may have had to do with the fact that you and I had shared a joint while in said car, waiting in the theater parking lot until it was time to go in and watch the movie.

We had chosen to see "Sling Blade", which I adored, and you slept through. When the lights came up and you woke up, you claimed it was one of the dumbest, most boring films you had ever seen.

I argued back that you hadn't actually seen more than about ten minutes of it. You claimed that it had been eight minutes more than you needed to come to that conclusion.

You always had strong opinions, and never once hesitated in sharing them. I adored you for that, even though your opinions could be rather harsh, to say the least. Do you remember when we would trade writing with each other for critiquing? Holy shit.

You could really hand out some criticism.

There you would be at your house in the country, sitting across from me in your soft, pink turtleneck with a pastel shawl draped over your slender shoulders, original dog at your feet, my pages clutched in your hand. Often, there was a fire in your fireplace. Out on your deck, colorful pots of blooming geraniums in fiery reds and pinks.

A pot of tea brewed and waiting to be poured.

Oh, what a calm and soothing environment in which to discuss writing. Oh, how looks can be deceiving.

"This is pure drivel," you stated one afternoon. "Drivel!" Come on, Jane. Tell me what you really think.

I had written a piece about having had two miscarriages and having had a dream about these tiny lost souls. I had written as if believing "they" were out there somewhere in the starry heavens.

I know, trite. But I was going for something. You were steaming.

"'They' aren't out there," you stated. "They" were just tissue and cells and that's it! "Don't be so sentimental in your writing," she continued.

"A being is only a being once it is born. Until then," you continued, "it is nothing. And after it dies, it is gone for good."

I knew you were right. And we then spent the late afternoon discussing life and when it actually does begin, and I copped to being overly sentimental about the two losses, and took my pages from you and crinkled them up, tossing them into the fire.

Between the two of us, we had laid out a clear and definite idea of what life is and how it begins and what happens when it is over. That the living must go on and that the dead are gone. There is no "after." Gone is gone. Move on. Get over it!

Simple. Easy.

Then you cloned your dog. Twice.

In the years since I have tried to reconcile that fact. Sadly, you have passed and, as far as I know, you have not been duplicated. I think you would have called if you had been.

The clones, as far as I know, are still around, humping, licking, chasing rabbits. And I am back to square one when it comes to understanding life and the Big Question of what happens next.

But oh, how I thank you, Jane, for expanding my perspective. For challenging me as a writer. And for allowing me the pleasure of cuddling with a clone.

xo Claudia

Jane, no last name, was a dear friend and fellow writer. She really did clone her dog and got two new pups out of the deal.

I have no idea how I feel about that.

Dear Joan Didion,

I am a long-time admirer of your work. I mean, who isn't? From the early stuff and up to the heartbreaking memoirs after you lost your husband. Your daughter.

A few years ago, I went with a friend to the 92nd Street Y in New York City to hear you speak and read from your book, "The Year of Magical Thinking". When you walked out on to the stage, I was struck by just how fragile you were. I realize you have always been quite slender, but this night you appeared as if a sneeze offered up by someone in the front row would knock you right over. I was worried about you.

You read from your book and then turned and began to leave the stage when a gentleman came out and whispered something to you. Apparently reminding you that you were to take questions.

I wanted him to let you go home and put on some flannel pajamas and climb into bed with a hot water bottle.

But he didn't. You turned back to the podium and in a very soft voice spoke for a bit and then departed the stage and were taken to a space where a table had been set up so that you might sign books for your enthusiastic readers.

My friend and I did not join the line. I really just wanted someone to get you home as quickly as possible so that you might, after tucking yourself into bed, have a big bowl of hot soup, I was thinking clam chowder, and a cocktail. I did not want to be part of the reason you were delayed. Even though I would have enjoyed expressing my thanks to you for your sharp-eyed observations and anger and wit.

In truth, I don't know if I would have even had the nerve to say anything to you. I admire you that much. My tongue may have tied in knots. My cheeks may have flamed.

When I returned to the apartment. I climbed into bed with a glass of red wine and a copy of your book and began reading it once again. Just seeing you had added depth to a memoir which was already as deep as the ocean and in many places just as dark and cold. I thought about you, back home just blocks away. It was a rainy night, cold and frigid, leaning towards snow I thought. I hoped you were warm and toasty. I read until I turned the last page, then turned out the light.

Oh, Joan, you are simply brilliant.

If I had queued up and made it to the front of the very long line, I am positive I would not have confessed to being a writer. You are a writer. How in the world could I possibly claim to be the same? Impossible!

Would a guy who painted porches tell Picasso that he too was a painter? While technically accurate, not really the same thing. Pablo would have clued him in.

But here is the funny thing, Joan. A few weeks later a memoir of mine was published. The booking person at the Y must not have noticed, as no invitation to speak came my way.

Also, there were no Broadway producers knocking on my door asking to turn it into a one-woman performance starring a member of the British acting community as respected as our own Meryl Streep. An honest to god Redgrave performing your words. I mean. come on. How thrilling must that have been?

However, my slim little book did receive some lovely and generous reviews. One of which was sent to me by a friend of my sister-in-law. This particular book review was the end-of-the-year roundup of "must reads" in "The Kansas City Star".

There were no big surprises in the fiction category. Many of their choices were also chosen by publications all around the country.

But, Joan, the lovely book editor at the Kansas City Star had drawn up a list of the 10 best memoirs of the year. And of course, "The Year of Magical Thinking" made the list. Then, and here is where it gets a bit unbelievable, my memoir also made their list. You and I, Joan Didion, shared a space on the page. Out of all the memoirs published that year, they chose yours and mine and acknowledged them. Praised them.

Holy shit!

I wanted to call you! I wanted to ask if you had seen the review. If you had decided to read the other nine books, mine among them, on the list.

I wrote the editors and thanked them. I didn't even know if that was the proper protocol, but what did I have to lose other than a cheery, Christmas-themed stamp.

Oh, Joan, I don't keep copies of everything I have ever written. I don't have copies of various reviews or letters: some praising my work, some not. I am simply not that organized. But I will never part with that "Kansas City Star" end-of-the-year review. Never. Because I can't imagine your name and my name will ever be on the same list again, (unless we book a reservation at the same restaurant for the same night and if I saw you, I would love to pick up the tab!), and there are times I don't actually believe it really happened and need to pull the now-beginning-to-yellow clip from my desk drawer and say, yes! It did happen!

When you saw it, were you as thrilled as I? Oh, I do hope so.

In the first few months after my younger sister died, I returned again and again to "The Year of Magical Thinking". You and I had suffered different losses, but our grief was so similar. I suppose hearts, when broken, do not vary all that much.

Oh, Joan, I do hope that the passage of time has been helpful to you and that you are now able to sleep through the night without disturbing dreams. I have not yet managed that feat. I wish we were neighbors. I wish we were friends. I wish we were close enough that if I saw your lights on at night I could pop over and knock on your door with a cup of hot tea or a bottle of Don Julio.

But all I can do at this point is (if I find myself wide awake in the middle of the night and get up to wander the house), send you my good wishes. Hope that you are tucked into a warm bed and are sleeping peacefully.

Pleasant dreams, Joan,
Claudia

Joan Didion was born in 1934 in Sacramento, California. She is known as a California writer, but also pens work about her life in New York City. There are some friends of mine who don't really get her, but I encourage them to stick with it. She is worth the effort!

She won the Pulitzer Prize for her autobiography, The Year of Magical Thinking. *During her long career, she has written plays, essays, films, novels, and memoirs. If you are unfamiliar with her work, or know her but want to know even more, check out the documentary on Netflix,* The Center Will Not Hold.

Seriously remarkable.

Dear Carol,

Did you know that in families of elephants the older sibling babysits the younger ones? And it appears they love each other forever.

Love,
Claude

Dear Carol,

Did you know that sister lions stay together their entire lives?

Love,
Claude

Dear Carol,

Did you know that Cattle Egrets, a kind of heron, will often kill their siblings while the parents are out looking for food? They don't want to share.

Love,
Claude

Dear Frank McCourt,

I could not believe the timing. You, author of one of my very favorite books, "Angela's Ashes", were coming to town to do a reading at one of our local book emporiums. Fate, and a booking agent, were delivering you to my doorstep, if you considered my doorstep to be downtown Santa Cruz which, technically, it is not. But still.

After reading the announcement in our local paper, I went to my kitchen calendar to circle the date.

The date was already circled. We had accepted an invitation to a bar mitzvah which would be at the same time. And I knew, even though the crowd at the celebratory gathering would be large and we may not even be missed if we were to duck out, I really didn't want to.

Oh, to have the ability to be in two places at the same time.

I was grumbly. Irritated at the terrible timing. We live in a fairly small town and here you were coming to visit and how often would that even happen and how unfair was it to have to miss it and grumble, grumble, grumble.

I had so many things I wanted to tell you. I wanted to express my deep admiration for your ability to tell a story, which had the power to make me cry and laugh at the exact same time!

I wanted to tell you that I adored your accent. That I had gone to one of your readings in New York City, but the line to greet you after was so long that I left before reaching the front, and that was after waiting for more than half an hour. I wanted to ask you just how you were able to keep the twinkle in your eye for an entire evening, especially when hands were raised and questions were asked, some of which were fairly asinine.

The morning of the event, both events actually, as I was tugging on a pair of pantyhose, hoping to smooth out my lumpy parts, my phone rang. It was the manager of the bookstore hosting your event. She wanted to know if I was going to be at your reading. I explained the situation and she paused, then issued an even better invitation. Would Michael and I like to come down to the store the next morning and Keep You Company (!!!) while you signed books?

Seriously. Would my husband and I like to hang out in the upstairs office of the store for a couple of hours and chat while you scrawled your name inside stacks and stacks of your memoir?

"We will be there with bells on," I promised.

"But, please," she asked. "Don't mention this to anyone."

That evening, while I imagined a large crowd gathered to hear you read and ask you questions, I danced my ass off at the party honoring a thirteen-year-old young man and knew I had scored big. And, as promised, I kept my secret to myself. Even when the host, knowing my love of you and your work, thanked me for choosing this event over yours.

The next morning, we drove downtown and parked the car. I had a copy of your book, which I hoped you might sign. Unbeknownst to me, Michael had tucked a copy of my first memoir in his backpack. I am still not sure how I feel about that, but do know I am glad I was unaware of his action.

We were ushered upstairs, and there you sat, stacks of books to your right, stacks of books to your left. Your "person" was with you. A young woman who I assume fetched your coffee or tea or jacket or scarf when you need them.

Your eyes still had that twinkle. I wondered if there was a particular eye wash that you used to achieve that look. Magic drops, available only in Ireland.

We were introduced and you seemed happy to have company while attending to all of the books.

I had so many questions, and yet I could not seem to make my brain send them to my vocal cords. I sat mute while Michael filled the silence with queries. And you, Mr. McCourt, told story after story.

By the time the last book had been inscribed, two hours had passed, and it was time to depart. I stood up and thanked you and you hugged me, telling me that it was you who were grateful for having had the company.

Then, Michael reached into his backpack and extracted my slim memoir and held it out to you.

"My wife wrote this," he stated.

I felt my throat constrict. My cheeks burned.

Before you could even take it, your person reached for it and offered to put it in your suitcase.

But here, Mr. McCourt, is where you made my day even more thrilling. You refused her offer, saying you would like to read it on the plane.

Really, Frank? Really?

That gracious move has stayed with me forever. My book may have been slight, but you did not want me to feel small.

And then our morning with you was over. Michael and I went out to breakfast and just stared at each other asking again and again: Did that just happen?

It had.

"What is it about McCourt as a writer that you love so much?" Michael asked me over home fries.

I'll tell you what I told him, Mr. McCourt. You showed me that a writer may write about the most horrific, heart-wrenching events in one paragraph, and then, by the next page, have the reader laughing out loud. You captured life as it happens and shared it with readers as if we were extended family. Your memoirs show both sides of the coin.

Michael kept nodding in agreement. I am not the only McCourt fan in the house.

A few years later, I was in New York and walking on the Upper West Side towards my favorite Sunday morning flea market. It is right behind the American Museum of Natural History. There is a row of apartment buildings across the street. I was just passing one when you stepped out of the lobby. You were with your wife.

I had always promised myself that if I ever had the chance to thank you, to actually speak to you, I would take it. I regretted my two hours of silence that long-ago morning. Well, there you both stood, and I was only steps away.

I called out your name and you turned and smiled.

A jumble of words filled my mouth, but before I let any of them escape, I knew I had to prioritize. What to say first so that you would not think I was a middle-aged lunatic or stalker.

I simply said that we had met in Santa Cruz and named the bookstore. It rang a small bell. You expressed fondness for the town and the store.

I told you how Michael and I had kept you company while you autographed books. Your face lit up. You did remember the morning.

You asked why I was in New York and where I was headed right then. I explained and then you asked if I would like to join you and your lovely wife for brunch.

I politely declined. I was completely done in from the unexpected encounter and knew in my heart of hearts that I would sit there mute if I decided to join you for pancakes and eggs.

I can only bear so much joy.

You never mentioned my book. I never mentioned it either. I wanted to hang on to the possibility that you had in fact read it on your journey home. That it was now tucked in between other favorite books on your shelves in your apartment. I am totally good with that.

And I just wanted to thank you for the grace you showed me. A beautiful example of how a writer who is quite high up the literary ladder might treat a writer who is too shy to even speak and is still perched on a much lower rung. And for proving without a shadow of a doubt that while life may have some really shitty moments and some overwhelming disappointments, there are also moments, if we keep our eyes open, which can make you laugh so hard you cry.

With admiration,
Claudia

P.S. You are gone now, but every time I pull one of your books from my shelf, you are back. You'll live forever.

Frank (Francis) McCourt was born in 1930 in, wait for it, Brooklyn, New York! In the middle of the Depression, his family moved back to Ireland where his parents had been born. By the time Frank moved back to the United States, he had acquired the delightful Irish accent he would carry with him until his last days.

He won the Pulitzer Prize for his memoir, Angela's Ashes, *and went on to write the memoir* 'Tis *as a followup. He then used his experiences teaching to write the fabulous memoir,* Teacher Man.

There was a film made of Angela's Ashes, *but really don't bother. There are no laughs in it anywhere. The book, however, found the perfect balance of tragedy and humor.*

Dear Emily Dickinson,

In reading your poetry and searching out information about you, I have never read anywhere that you ever spent time exploring the East Village in New York City. But, for my 60th birthday, I took you there. In spirit at least.

The East Village can be a bit gritty, but nothing like it once was. These days there are tourists, hipsters, cafes with coffee served in as many ways as one could possibly imagine, vintage shops, bars, some dive, but mostly not, and tattoo parlors. Ink has become very, very popular. And this, Miss Emily, is what brought me to the colorful neighborhood on a Tuesday evening a few summers ago. My daughter was with me. She, who has lots of experience when it comes to ink, was there to cheer me on. I was about to get body art. My first, if piercing doesn't count. I mean who, these days, doesn't have their ears pierced, other than my friend Christy.

Although I was a tattoo virgin, it was not my first time in a parlor. The day my daughter turned 18, a day I had imagined taking her to high tea at the Plaza Hotel, she had other ideas in mind.

"I'm getting a tattoo today because I can," she declared first thing in the morning. She also stated that she would be purchasing porn and cigarettes, again because she could. She desperately wished there was an election taking place, so she might cast her ballot. I had two choices, neither of which would dissuade her. I could be a part of her birthday celebration or let her go on her own.

Oh, Emily, you, never having had children, may think I did in fact have another option. I could stop her. Tell her just how un-ladylike tramp stamps are and lecture her on the fact that her taste would surely change and she would regret this early-morning decision for the rest of her life.

I could take away her cell phone. Disconnect the internet. Ban "The Real Housewives" from our television. Oh, my dear, how the world has changed since you sent poems down by basket to those waiting beneath your window.

Well, Miss Em, parenting is filled with challenges. Battles to be fought and won and fought and lost and I chose not to pull rank on her. I instead chose to join her on her adventure. I held her hand as she stretched out on a table face down and had a sun/moon drama mask inked onto her lower back.

Now, here we were, years later making an appointment with a tattoo artist so that each of us could acquire new ink. I have lost count of how many decorations my daughter has, but for me, this would be my first.

Our wait was short, and we both knew exactly what we wanted and where. My daughter, who is far from warm and fuzzy, more prickly pear, surprised me by her sentimentality. When she was a small child, she was shy. "Uppie me," she would beg if she was feeling timid. And I would hoist her up and set her on my hip where she felt safe.

This is what she wanted written forever on her body. "Uppie Me." On her hip. In my handwriting. I didn't tell her how touched I was. She undoubtedly would have changed her mind.

Then it was my turn.

My artist was a bearded chap with colorful designs covering most of his dermis. He also had what looked like black rubber discs embedded in his earlobes. (It's a style these days, Em. Again, a lot has changed.)

He asked if I had been drinking. I told him not yet. Good, he replied.

He had a rule about never tattooing anyone who had been imbibing. There could be excessive bleeding. Or excessive feelings of regret the next day, and why should he have to deal with a bloody, hungover, angry customer?

He asked me where I wanted the tattoo. I believe he may have held his breath as he waited for my answer. I mean, at 60, there are only so many places on my being which should be seen by men I don't even know. Even professionals.

I pointed to my wrist.

His shoulders dropped ever so slightly as he let out his breath and relaxed. He then asked me what I wanted.

When I told him, he was unfamiliar with the quote.

It was then that I introduced him to you, Emily Dickinson. He had heard of you, but did not know you.

He practiced on paper before piercing my skin. His cursive was lovely. I was surprised. These days it is no longer taught in school. That, Miss Emily, hurts my heart. I can't imagine what you would say were you to visit us here in this century and discover that most of those lovely swirls and dips and circles you used to write your poetry in would be foreign to young students today.

I digress.

I was enjoying my time in this environment. There was a large gentleman in the booth next to me lying on a table having work done on his chest. Part of his design included a massive set of wings which I thought would look better on his back, as it seems as if that is where you might find wings was kind of a coincidence, as wings figured into my plan for my own tattoo, and his torso was in grave danger of looking as busy as the wallpaper my auntie Di once had in her dining room if he continued to go under the needle.

I approved the design I was shown by Eric (I felt I should know his name as this was feeling a bit intimate), and placed my arm on the wide, flat arm of the chair.

Soon I developed a great admiration for the gentleman next to me. How the fuck (pardon my language, but we are in a tattoo parlor), was he able to take it?

Thirty minutes later, we were finished. We paid up and trotted across the street to the nearest establishment serving tequila. My wrist was wrapped in gauze bandages.

Later, after dropping off my daughter, my taxi pulled up in front of the apartment and our doorman Jose released me from my yellow cab and then opened the door to the lobby. The lights seemed extra bright. In the glare, he noticed my wrapped wrist. Then noticed my wobbly stance.

"You didn't ..." he began.

"I did!" I replied.

"What does it say?" he asked.

Carefully, I unwrapped the bandage and held up my wrist to be examined.

"Hope is the Thing", it read. With a cerulean blue feather drawn delicately beneath the cursive writing.

He gave me a gentle high five.

In the years since, I have introduced you to many others. A bartender at Phil's Fish Market in Moss Landing, California. A sales clerk at Filene's Basement before they went out of business, a punky looking gentleman on the 6 train, a woman seated at the next table in Manuel's Mexican restaurant in Aptos, California, and my grandson, who, at only 4 years of age, is restricted to stick-on tattoos for now.

So, I thank you, Emily. I have carried the words in my heart and relied on them often. Now I wear them, not on my sleeve, but on my person. My daughter and I were not alone downtown on those once-gritty streets. You, in your virginal white, were with us for inspiration.

I'd love to know what you thought of it all!

Fondly,
Claudia

Emily Dickinson was born in Amherst, Massachusetts in 1830 and died in 1886. (I thought everyone knew her, but since tatting myself with words I always attribute to her, I have learned differently. What is being taught in school these days?)

As a young woman, she studied at the Amherst Academy for seven years. She then dipped her toe in the world of Mount Holyoke Seminary, but quickly returned to the family home in Amherst.

Neighbors thought she was a bit off. Dressed in all white most of the time, she spent her days writing poetry — much of which was never published while she was alive.

She was known to stay hidden away in her room and apparently avoided people like the plague.

She never witnessed her own success. But she became so very popular that one woman even had a small piece of her poetry tattooed on her wrist more than a century after her passing!

Dear Carol,

This morning I remembered a call from you. It was years ago. I was in my kitchen and the phone rang. When I answered it, the person on the other end identified themselves as a publisher. A book publisher! They were calling to offer me my first publishing deal. My first book was going to be in book stores! In libraries!

I was thrilled. Beside myself. And, using that phrase, I find I actually mean it. It was like I was out of my own body and standing next to me staring at the happy, half-demented woman hanging on the phone.

A book I had written was to be PUBLISHED!

First, I called Michael. He said he would buy a bottle of Champagne on his way home. The phone rang again and I picked it up expecting it to be Michael with an even more exciting plan. Dinner out?

But it was you. And you were crying. Before I could even tell you my news, you told me you had a lump in your neck. That a doctor told you it might be cancer. That you were terrified.

I'll call in sick at work. I'll come up tomorrow, I told you. Then I called Michael and cancelled the Champagne.

It turned out not to be cancer, but many days passed before we found out. Only then did I tell you about the book deal. But that seemed so inconsequential after what we had gone though in the previous days.

You called me. You needed me.

Remember?

Of course, there would be another phone call just a handful of years later when you were told that you had cancer, this time for sure. And again, I drove up and over the mountain which separated my house from yours and was there.

So, the point of this?

It is true we never had a relationship which led to chatting on the phone every day about books or friends, or fashion or politics, but when something really frightened you, you remembered our birth order. I was your older sister.

So you called. Thank you for that.

It is interesting to find what, after years of missing you, I hang onto. You, reaching out to me in times where you were terrified, gives me some small measure of comfort. I would give anything if you could reach out once more to remind me of your love. Five minutes, one minute, thirty seconds, anything.

Call me.

Forever yours,
Claude

Dear Patricia Polacco,

It was in a small book store in Berkeley that I first discovered you. It was in the Elmwood neighborhood and I was strollering my daughter when a book in their window caught my eye. The title was "The Keeping Quilt". And it was a children's book. We strollered in. It was the beginning of a beautiful relationship.

Paying full price for a hard cover book was a luxury. We lived on a tight budget, and I felt a twinge of guilt as I handed over the money. But the discomfort melted away as I began to read the book out loud to my daughter. The story, as you know, was about a family who had immigrated to this country with very little. They were Jewish, just as my husband is. His family came from Europe at about the same time yours did.

Over time, the cover of the book became quite tattered due to the fact that it was read so very often. I began to watch for new books written and illustrated by you. I began to watch for announcements about readings you might be giving. I became such a fan that a friend gave me a gift certificate for a writing workshop you were giving in Marin County. It was a life-changing day for me. I do not say that lightly. I was just beginning my own career as a writer and you encouraged me to go on. But this thank-you letter isn't really about that. I just couldn't write to you without mentioning it.

Back to you and your own writing.

I have no idea how many times I took my daughter to see you read from your latest publication. One afternoon, I took her out of school early, along with her best friend, and we drove from Santa Cruz to Oakland where you were performing at a cozy little book store not far from where you actually lived at the time. I am not a stalker; I only know your house was nearby because you mentioned it at the reading.

We arrived in time to secure seats close to the front, and your books, with their lush illustrations, were on display everywhere. I realized I was going to have another one of those guilty moments before leaving the store because I didn't see how I could possibly turn my back on books written by you that I didn't own already.

I soothed myself with the fact that the store threw in a free book bag.

The book you were promoting that afternoon was "Pink and Say". It was the story of two young men during the Civil War. It was a remarkable tale that reached its climax with the phrase, "This is the hand that has touched the hand that has touched the hand that shook the hand of Abraham Lincoln."

Well.

Then you went around to the children in the room and while repeating those lines, shook their hands.

By the time we got home that night, both my daughter and her best friend were repeating your words, but simplifying the statement. Soon they were saying they met Abraham Lincoln. Adorable.

Over the years, I continued to watch for your latest contributions to the children's canon of literature. Even after my own girl grew up and moved on with her life. Last week, my grandson came to stay and I read him one of your stories. I chose "Mrs. Katz and Tush". An abandoned kitten is part of the story and we have had a wandering cat stopping by once or twice a day, which thrills my Darling Boy. He has named the cat Sweet Baboo. A new tradition has begun. I couldn't have imagined it that Sunday afternoon when I first discovered you in Berkeley.

But in truth, this thank you note isn't really about the joy you have given my daughter or now her son, although you deserve my deepest gratitude for all of those hours of entertainment. This is about my mother.

Over the past couple of years, my mother has lost more and more of her "faculties." Where once she read newspapers and books, she now flips pages of People Magazine and is confused by the headlines, never mind the articles. She has no interest in what has been written about the latest "Star Wars" movie or the newest "Planet of the Apes" film.

Every week when I would walk into her room in her assisted living facility and see the magazines, I would feel terrible that this was the best she was offered, but I was unsure what I could come up with as an alternative.

Do you see where I am headed?

I have now introduced my mother to your books! Even if she gets lost in the text, she is cheered by the artwork. Her caregivers love the stories too! One asked if she could borrow a book to take home for her child to read. I told her yes, but made her promise to return it to my mother.

It feels as though this is some kind of full circle moment. I have read your books to my own child, then my grandchild, and now my mother is comforted and entertained by your writing. She especially loves "Chicken Sunday". She is captivated by the tale of the culturally-mixed neighborhood and the friendships the children develop. She says it reminds her of our old Oakland neighborhood, and how we all played in the streets until it was too dark to even see.

I am sure there will come a day when even your books will be too much for her to grasp. But for now, a new world has opened for my mother. Your world!

Oh, dear Patricia, I thank you for being the writer you are. Your gift of being able to tell a story that all ages can appreciate. Even folks in their 80s.

Ever grateful,
Claudia

Patricia Polacco was born in 1944 in Michigan. She is a writer/illustrator of fantastic children's books. She is amazingly prolific and uses much of her own life in her stories. She is so popular, has such a strong following, that she hosts a gathering at her farm each year and hundreds — perhaps thousands — of devoted fans fill the local hotels and motels to spend the day with her.

I don't blame them.

If you have ever been a child, know a child, love a child, check out her books. Seriously fantastic!

Dear Carol,

It has been months since you left us and I am still struggling. I emailed Cheryl yesterday. Just a short note. I asked her if you felt about me the same as your wife. And if your friends shared those feelings. I wanted her to write back so that if the news was unpleasant, I could read it slowly, just a little at a time. But instead, she called.

"Are you ready for the truth?" Cheryl asked. I told her yes.

It was like a knife.

You have all felt the same for a very long time.

I did not see that coming. The nightmare grows and grows.

I cried and asked Cheryl why she hadn't just emailed me this news rather than call. Sisters don't talk about love in an email she replied.

I could not find the love in what she was saying. I was listening hard, but didn't even hear a hint of love or affection.

This is a setback.

I will try not to spend the rest of my life wondering why. Wondering exactly when it was that I lost you both.

If she could have just given me one thing. Something solid to explain why you have felt this way, it would help. But all I am told is that I am different. That I am dramatic. I asked again for clarification on that. When am I dramatic?

She can't really give me an example other than right now and over the past few months. But it is dramatic to lose one's sisters. It is a nightmare. I am feeling it.

I am sorry if my heartbreak is showing.

Love,
Claude

P.S. I do know my emotions run close to the surface. They break through often, leaping trout in a stream. Visible from the shore. If I were to describe your wife's emotions using the same metaphor, I would say the stream had frozen over, trapping any life below. Perhaps the cold, smooth surface is easier to live with?

Dear Carol,

It is late and I'm in bed. I can hear the fireworks going off at Dodger Stadium. Your niece lives fairly close to the ballpark. I never know if the popping and snapping and booming means that a run has been scored or what. But I like listening to the celebration from my bed in my Darling Boy's room.

Baseball makes me think of being outside at Auntie Di and Uncle Charlie's house when we were kids. Do you remember how we would spend all afternoon in their pool and the Giant's game would be on the radio and Auntie Di would make fruit salad and use the melon baller to make perfectly round, seedless orbs of watermelon, cantaloupe, and honeydew? Our bellies would be as bloated and round as those melons by the end of the day. Then it would be time to leave, and Ma would load our stuff in the car. We would argue about who got to sit in front for the drive home. We took turns.

If I had ridden up next to Ma on the way, then you and Cheryl got the front going home. I never thought of splitting you up. I guess Ma didn't either.

It's funny how one can mean one, but in the case of twins, two can also seem like one.

When you knew you were dying, when you began to give away your possessions, your leather coat to sweet Jennifer, your car to Cheryl, did you give your twin to your wife so she would still be one rather than one half? If you had told me you were going to, I would have understood. I would have volunteered for the position of other half, but I would have understood if you chose differently.

It's the not knowing that is so hard. Logic tells me that after losing you, Cheryl would have turned to me. But she didn't. Was this the plan? If you had let me know I would have prepared myself. I would have been comforted by the fact that my remaining sister was simply taking care of herself. I want her to be okay.

I suppose I have to stop thinking of her as my little sister. She is a grown woman with children and grandchildren and is fully capable of taking care of herself. But I still remember both of you as hardly more than babies. Running through the house, climbing up on the kitchen counters to reach the cupboard doors to remove anything that struck your fancy.

I remember the three of us taking our pillows and using them as sleds to bump down the flight of stairs that led to the basement. I remember all of the tents we made. The tents were filled with comic books and sleeves of saltine crackers, a jar of peanut butter and pillows and blankies and love. Weren't they?

I have gotten myself into a state now. I am going to go quietly downstairs, no sledding with pillows, and make myself a drink. Tequila with grapefruit juice and a squeeze of lime.

My friend Christy says I am drinking too much. But she still has all of her sisters and you have been gone for six months.

So, what does she know?

Love,
Claude

Dear Darling Boy,

You are about to arrive!

It is a Thursday night. Your dad has arrived home from Germany where he was shooting a movie. Michael, soon to be known as Pops, has arrived from Santa Cruz. It looks as if you will arrive tomorrow.

Pops and I have checked into a hotel with a pool and a delightful Happy Hour. Drinks for $5.00! Shrimp for $5.00! We are happy! We sit and watch vacationers frolic in the pool. I am too tired to frolic physically, but mentally I am doing the tango. Excited, because back at the apartment are your mom and dad waiting to become a family of three.

I love being with Pops again. It has been almost three weeks and I have to say it is quite sexy sitting around a pool in LA sipping tequila and eating shrimp with a soon-to-be grandfather. You will see that he is handsome for an old dude. His once dark beard is now flecked with white. His once long dark hair is shorn close to the scalp. In some places all there is, is scalp.

I don't know how I became so lucky. We have been together more than 30 years and there have been the usual pot holes and unexpected tsunamis, but also so much beauty.

Darling Boy, I hope you have a life filled with adventure. We have!

Living in the tropics for a year eating barracuda, giving birth to a girl, your mama, who, from her first second, seemed to be on her own path. Sitting in theaters in New York and L.A. and London, watching her on stage.

Sitting on our front porch swing sharing a cigarette and a Scotch. (We were paying homage to the book "The Bridges of Madison County", a book you will most likely never read! Also, never smoke!)

Waking up next to each other on a Saturday morning, hundreds of Saturday mornings, and staying put. Breakfast in bed. Coffee. Newspapers spread everywhere. It has been a lifetime filed with unexpected pleasure. Often actual, honest-to-god bliss. And now we get you. Our fantastical, miracle Darling Boy.

Thank you for making the trip!

Love,
Claudia (Your Mimi)

Dear Carol,

He is here. He is a star fallen from the sky. He is healthy and looks exactly like his parents. His skin is the color of ripe apricots.

Ripe apricots!

He is going to have an amazing life.

No one knows it yet, but in just two weeks the family of three will be moving to New York City where the father has taken another job. This time for television. It is a great job. But they may be gone for 6 months.

We will all deal with it. There are planes flying all day every day. We all may as well get used to it.

You know I am not a believer. But still I wonder if you can somehow see them. If you can visit without having to purchase a plane ticket or go through those long security lines.

I also want you to know that I have no doubt that, even though you and Cheryl may not have liked me (oh that sounds so junior high), I think there still was some kind of strong bond. Something forged when we were small. In our tent in our room. Something buried deep in our hearts that is still there. A diamond in a mine.

I wish we all three could go back to our childhood home and stand in the backyard under the wide oak tree and remember the three blonde girls who played in the sprinkler, climbed on the jungle gym, made our way to the roof of the garage, and picked apples from the neighbor's tree while their dog, Archie, barked and howled.

I wish we could go back and build one more tent, climb inside, and find those three little girls. The Nielsen girls. We loved each other then. Didn't we?

Love,
Claude

Dear Don Julio,

You and I have become a little too close over the past few months. It may be time to reevaluate our relationship.

Oh, I am not thinking of cheating on you with another, perhaps lesser brand of tequila, but I am thinking I should probably try drinking my grapefruit juice straight once in a while, rather than with a big old splash of you.

Please don't panic. This is not a full-on breakup. Just a tiny time out.

I have been using you. Relying on you to soothe my nerves. Leaning on you for comfort. But I am afraid if I continue to do, so I will be so "comforted" that I pass out at my desk.

Plus, you don't always cheer me up. Often, I pass "comfort" and slide right into a sob sister. No fun for anyone.

(Right now, let me shout out a big thank you to my friend Becky for extracting me from the Italian restaurant where our book club was meeting and where I had been drinking and I lost control of my emotions after one of my friends asked about Cheryl and if I had seen her or talked to her and I melted into a puddle of sadness. Thanks B!)

So, Julio, as fond as I am of you and always will be, I am going to step back just a bit. I am not going to give you up completely, but we will not be hanging out every single day. Think of it as becoming my "special" friend. You know, someone whom one looks forward to spending time with because it is a rare occasion, rather than just a friend one sees every day and soon takes for granted.

Think of yourself as Santa Claus, as opposed to the perfectly nice mail delivery person who every day brings me junk mail, requests for donations and bills.

Please don't think I don't adore you. I do. Mucho. I expect I always will!

Gracias,
Claudia

Don Julio is actually a real person! He began crafting his tequila in 1942 at the age of 17. A real go-getter was Don Julio Gonzalez-Frausto Estrada!

Yes, there are many different tequilas on the market, including one created by heart throb George Clooney, which I have yet to try, but Don Julio's is my favorite. And until Mr. Clooney knocks on my door with a free bottle and a sack of limes, I'm sticking with you.

Dear Carol,

You have been gone for more than two years now. It feels as if there have been so many secrets. Did you keep secrets when you were young? I mean we all did, but did you and Cheryl share secrets? Big, large secrets that felt like a burden? Bushel baskets filled with stones, which had to be carried all day and stuffed under the bed at night?

What were you afraid to tell me?

Do you remember when you were sick the first time and one night as I lay next to you in your bed, you said you had something you needed to say. You were speaking about the woman you had been living with for years and would continue to live with until the day you died.

"She is my dearest friend," you whispered. You were crying.

I waited for more. But you were silent then, just staring deep into my eyes. I told you that I knew. Of course I knew. She was your person, just as Michael is mine and Howie is Cheryl's. But something kept you from just saying that.

My dearest friend. It sounded almost Victorian. And I knew you wanted me to understand the meaning behind the term, but it felt as if someone else had shaped your words. Someone else had guided your confession. As if I were not to be trusted with the truth of your relationship.

It would be 12 years later that you would call me to say you were getting married. Something I felt you had been all along. She was the love you had been waiting for. I was so happy you had found your mate. You belonged to someone and she to you. I did not know at the time there were strings attached. That for her to accept you completely, you would have to disavow me. Perhaps that was the bargain struck. She would tolerate me when she had to, but never accept me. And it was your duty to see me through her eyes.

I wish you could have told me that. We might have developed a secret code where, when all together, I would know that you were still my sister, you loved me and, if at times you acted unlike yourself, I would know it was just the way the game was being played.

Everyone in a relationship makes allowances for their partner. They give up garlic or onions, or sleep on the side of the bed they aren't used to, or agree to get a puppy even though they are really cat people.

If you had said to me years ago, "Claude, I love her, but you drive her nuts, so pay no attention to how I may act around you, it is to keep the peace," I would have said fine. Then we could have worked out a code.

But maybe, as you listened to her complain about me, your love for her was so deep and strong you were swept away in her river of hate. Not to the point where you too hated me, but to where you had to hold tight to her words in order not to drown. Like foul-smelling little life preservers. Not exactly what you might have wanted, but in order to keep afloat, you just had to pinch your nose and hang on.

Is this what happened?

I will have to figure it out. But I am at least asking the questions. Making my list. Oh, to have 30 minutes with you once more. Alone.

Love,
Claude

Dear Steve Jobs,

I own an Apple computer. I own an Apple phone, though not the latest. I may have one app, but I'm not sure. I never thought I would be writing to thank you for anything. I am just not a techie. However, last week I would have baked you a cake or sent you a dozen donuts, if you were still able to receive such gifts. A full baker's dozen!

So, why am I reaching out to you? Why am I so grateful to a man who oversaw the creation of so many devices I really don't have that much interest in?

Imagine you are in a small blue car seated next to a three-year-old and driving down California's Highway 5 from Santa Cruz to Los Angeles. Imagine all is well for the first three and a half hours. Pops is in the driver's seat. I am in charge of toddler entertainment. Small toys have been played with. Books have been looked at. A role of Scotch tape has been fiddled with. Stickers have been placed on the blank dinosaurs' faces in the Giant Dino Sticker Book.

A banana has been consumed. Some raisins and cranberries have been snacked on. A breakfast bar has gone down the hatch. Songs have been sung. Fields of strawberries have been pointed out, as have fields of lettuce and rows of grapes.

I'm watching for signs of a possible nap. Surely, he must be tired. Kids sleep in the car. Especially on such long car rides.

Except when they don't.

But wait. Just as we are passing the never tempting outlet mall at the foot of the Grapevine, I see his head dip. Quickly, he rights himself, only to nod once again. The weight of his head too much it seems.

And he is out!

I give a thumbs-up in the mirror to Pops and lean back in my seat ready to enjoy some down time.

And then he is up. Really up. Fifteen minutes into what I thought might be a two-hour slumber, which would have landed us right at his mama's door.

He is not happy. Really not happy. His screams drown out the sounds of giant semis cranking up the hill next to our little blue car.

So, okay, I undid my seatbelt. I attempted to wrap myself around his car seat in a kind of weird hug.

He wants the window down. It is 100 degrees out and we are now driving at about 70 miles per hour.

I try to have an intelligent conversation with him about the downside of a downed window under these conditions. He is not impressed with my logic.

His blond hair is becoming matted and his face is crimson and dripping with tears. My phone pings. MY PHONE!

"Darling Boy," I ask. "Do you want to see a video? Do you want to see lots of videos?" He is still crying, but does not say no.

I am curled around his car seat like a snake curls around inside a basket. My left hand is resting on the floor of the car, my elbow locked, supporting me as I try to snuggle closer, to soothe him.

With my right hand, I touch the screen of my device and bring up photos and videos from months back. Years back. I select one from my Darling Boy's one-year doctor visit. I remember the day. It was in Brooklyn, in the heat of summer. My daughter and I strollered him from their apartment to the medical building. The waiting room was filled with strollers, babies, mothers, and fathers. We waited our turn and, when invited into an examination room, noticed there was a mirror placed on the wall about two feet off the ground. Darling Boy placed both hands on the mirror and began to play a game of peek-a-boo with himself. I filmed it with my phone, never imagining I would use it as a major distraction two years later driving down to L.A.

We watched short films of my Darling Boy watching the Warriors play and cheering for his favorite player, Stephen Curry. He watched his friend Sam, younger by just a few months, try to navigate a slide.

His screaming stopped. His breathing became regular. He asked to see more. My arm was fully asleep. I didn't care.

We traveled through time watching him grow from newborn to a three-year-old who now knows how to use the potty and peddle a small tractor. From an infant with no verbal skills to speak of to a little boy who rarely stops talking. And there it all was, right at my fingertips. In my phone!

Steve, were you so forward thinking that you imagined this exact scenario? Is that why you created this new technology? Did you picture long, hot car rides with really cranky kids who could be calmed and soothed by watching movies of themselves on a tiny screen? Genius!

My phone is capable of much, although I have only explored about 10% of what it can do. I still have no understanding of The Cloud. But I know this. I can take pictures and make videos and save them. I can find them with one hand while the other is pressed to the floor of the car and a child is beet red with frustration. And, like music can soothe the savage beast, short films have the power to calm a raging child strapped in a carseat.

And I can FaceTime!

Which I am going to do right now to see just what my little darling might be up to.

In your debt,
Claudia

Steven Jobs was born in 1955 and died in 2011. He was, depending on your view point, a brilliant inventor, or a monster attempting to dominate the world. I still have not decided which side of the argument I fall on. He created things we now can't live without. Which is the problem. I do have an Apple Computer and I use an Apple device for a phone. But I hate that I now depend on so many of his inventions!

Dang, did he improve the world, or just open up a can of worms that we can never put the lid on?

But, oh, how I love to FaceTime my Darling Boy.

Dear Ina Garten,

Or do you prefer "The Barefoot Contessa"?

It is a Sunday afternoon and I am getting ready to have company for a barbecue in our backyard. The lawn is completely dead (the California drought), but I have a big, long table covered with woven multi-colored tablecloths. I took my red ceramic pitcher and filled it with water and the last of our beautiful hydrangeas to use as a centerpiece. I am going to grill swordfish (your recipe!) and ribs (again, your instructions!) and I have made the corn salad that my sister used to love.

I believe you would be impressed!

Guests will be here in an hour and now I am crying. I keep thinking about all of the parties I have had in our yard. How my family would all come down for the day and we would sit in back under the shade of umbrellas when the sun was overhead, and then later in the afternoon, in the shade of the redwoods and oaks.

When my younger sisters, twins, turned 50, I threw them a birthday party here. I turned my red kitchen chairs into thrones for the two of them, bedecked with ribbons and garlands of flowers. I had flowered headpieces made for them each to wear. And there were goodie bags with squirt guns and bubbles and who knows what.

Oh, Ina. I think you would have enjoyed it!

I invited friends of mine who just wanted to celebrate my sisters.

I made your peach and raspberry crisp, as well as your pecan squares for the occasion. I have pictures of that day all over my house. Taped inside the kitchen cupboards. Mounted on the refrigerator door.

I keep seeing them today as I prepare for another party. But this time without my family. That makes me sad.

The pictures will stay up though. They remind me that, yes, there was good. That happiness was right in my own backyard.

Many thanks, Ina, for all of the inspiration and your can't-fail recipes!

Claudia

P.S. Today I am making your outrageous brownies which I know will be a huge success. Also, if you don't look down at the brown and brittle lawn, it still looks beautiful out back. That might be a good philosophy for life. Don't look down.

Ina Garten was born in 1948 and is still cookin'. She is a prolific cook book author and hosts a cooking show on the Food Network called The Barefoot Contessa. *She creates fantastic meals for friends and for her husband, Jeffery, who always looks very happy and well-fed.*

When she clangs the dinner bell, everyone comes running. I would too if I were in the neighborhood.

Dear Carol,

It has been almost four years since you left us, and I am still haunted by the events that surrounded your death. I woke this morning and remembered the sound of the phone ringing that day very early. I knew exactly what it was, but tried not to rise to the surface to face what was coming. If I could remain deep in sleep, then you would not be gone. If I could shut my eyes to the light and my ears to the sound you would still be here.

Please, don't make me come to the surface. Please.

Michael's voice was calm. The conversation brief. Then he hung up and looked at me. "I'm sorry," he said and then wrapped his arms around me.

It was Cheryl who had called. She asked if I would break the news to our mother and in person. Would we drive up to their house and tell them?

Oh Carol, I don't remember taking a shower or getting dressed, but once in the car I realized they would want to have some food around the house for friends or family who may stop in. Or even just for themselves. So, we drove over to Gayle's in Capitola. You used to love to go there to eat. I chose pastries from the baked goods case and prepared foods from the refrigerated section. Meatloaf and mashed potatoes. Roast chicken. Lasagna. Roasted vegetables and sourdough bread.

While waiting to pay, two men ahead of me got to bickering about whose turn it was to be waited on. Neither would back down. My nerves were raw. My stomach churning as they fought for the right to be first.

I wanted to interrupt them and tell them why I was in line so early with so much food. I wanted them to know that you had died only a few hours earlier, and that just because the world was continuing to turn and they were still breathing, they didn't need to spend their precious time on the planet arguing over the space they occupied in line.

I didn't. I felt Michael's arm as he gripped mine.

He shook his head. I kept my silence. The clerk sorted it all out.

Off we drove, up and over the mountain to break the terrible, yet expected news. And we did.

Here's the thing, Carol, I wanted to know everything about that morning. Your last hours.

I wanted to be able to see exactly what happened. I wanted a complete, detailed narrative. Were you alone? Was the night nurse there? Who took your body downstairs? Where were your wife and our sister? Did they turn their backs as you were taken from the house? Did they escort you to the ambulance? Did they stand in the kitchen looking out at the garden? The water? The geese flying low.

What I wanted, dearly, desperately, overwhelmingly, was to have been there. I wanted to have looked into your eyes as you realized it was coming. I wanted to hold you and comfort you as you drifted away. I wanted to whisper in your ear until your breath was still.

So now, all this time later, I am sending you my love. My gratitude. Is it pointless? Can you feel it?

Please?

Love,
Claude

Dear Real Housewives of Beverly Hills,

Okay, so I can't imagine any of my friends confessing that they watch your Bravo show. But I am here to say that you ladies, and I use the term loosely in some of your cases, really helped me through a rough patch. Seriously.

Days after an unexpected surgery for a collapsed large intestine (and let me say that is a fucked-up experience), and finally home in my own bed, now missing eight inches of said intestine along with my appendix, I was too tired and on too many pain meds to make any sense at all of the written word. And to add to my situation, that day, after I got home from the hospital, my mother died. My mind was a wreck. My mood dark and dank.

I had a big stack of books on my nightstand and none of them made a lick of sense to me. And not that these books were particularly highbrow, but they were of a high enough quality that I would not be ashamed if one of my friends popped by and saw them. What to do?

I contemplated following Donald Trump on Twitter, but then realized that that would mean I had given up on life completely. Take me out back and chuck me over the fence and let the raccoons feed on my body.

My daughter called me from Los Angeles one morning and asked how I was. I told her I couldn't concentrate on anything. Nothing seemed to stick.

Try the "Housewives", she advised. She swore I would not have to struggle to make sense of any of it and, that if I forgot it all, it didn't matter. She suggested "Beverly Hills". Well, my dears, you hooked me. Your houses, your jewels, your shoes and bags, your facelifts, your hair extensions, your fluffy lips and fluffy little dogs and miniature horses! Your breasts! Your cars! Your parties where always, always there would be a blistering tongue-lashing by at least one of you.

Your ability to gossip and then forget completely what you had said and whom you had trashed! Fabulous!

I do not judge. I do not envy. But I became addicted. Kim and Kyle, will you ever repair your sisterly bond? Lisa, will you ever allow others to wear pink?

And just a general question: Is it ever appropriate for one to drive a $250,000 rose gold Bentley convertible to volunteer at a soup kitchen?

And what about you Yolanda? You claimed to love your husband so much that you were happy to treat him like a king. You live in a Malibu mansion fit for a queen! Do you ever feel it is too good to be true?

Spoiler alert, it is.

And the other Lisa, the lippy one. Man, do you like to stir the pot. Will you ever be busted for it?

I'm telling you, ladies, you made the time fly by and I am grateful.

At one point, I feel I sank to my lowest. I had one window open on my laptop so I could watch you and a second window open so I could shop on eBay. Shallow much?

When I watched Pink Lisa try on a pink diamond ring worth more than my house, I was proud of myself that I didn't begin searching for deal on diamonds on the discount site. I showed some restraint. Plus, I tried to imagine explaining my purchase of big bling to my husband or even my friends.

"Yes, I know we only have one small bathroom in our 1,000 sq. foot house and the driveway needs resurfacing and we need a new dishwasher, but I really thought I needed a ring the size of my now missing appendix to feel complete."

I did click the Buy button when I came across a baby-pink leather jacket, however. I am not perfect!

I kept you a secret from my pals. I did not try to convert them into watchers of wives. But now that I am up and about, and have stepped away from the screen and can read the New York Times, as well as books of a middlebrow level, I am coming out of the closet, which is about one-tenth the size of any of yours, to tell you all how much you helped me. I'm telling my friends as well!

But here is an interesting fact. Over the years I have come to see and hear things about the housewives of Beverly Hills. Standing in line at the grocery store and reading tabloid headlines, grabbing a People magazine at the airport before boarding a flight, or even catching an episode on said flight. I know things about your lives that, when watching the early seasons, you did not know were coming. This gave me a powerful feeling when watching. I could predict your future.

Here is a young woman married to a man who seems a little standoffish and perhaps stressed. She is struggling with her relationship. I know what her future holds. Her husband kills himself.

Or another wife who is married to a famous actor and is struggling to maintain a relationship with him while he is working in NYC. I know what is coming. An ugly divorce.

Then there is the couple who own a basketball team and properties in Los Vegas and bicker like three-year-olds all day, every day.

The end of a marriage is coming.

One of you, after sharing the view from your closet, which is as big and abundant as a department store, will come home to find that your closet has been cleaned out by thieves. Every bag, piece of jewelry, every red-soled pair of shoes.

On and on. There were shit storms a-waiting for you girls, even though on the surface you seem to have it all.

It leads one to wonder, would you want to know what is ahead?

I remember back to when I was in my 20s and beginning a new career as a flight attendant with the world at my feet and my future unknown. Could I ever have imagined what that future would be? Would I have signed up for it?

I suppose it is better to live in the dark and hope for the best. But it is tempting to try to see what is over the horizon.

There have even been episodes where you women have asked psychics to give you a peek at what is to come. But would you really want to know?

What I wouldn't give to sit down with you and, while sipping on a chilled rosé, ask you. In any case, I thank you all for helping me get through a rough patch that I never saw coming.

Double air kisses to you all, Darlings,
Claudia

The Real Housewives of Beverly Hills. *This is a Bravo "reality" show, which began in 2010 and continues to this day. The cast does change from time to time and, in truth, many of the women aren't housewives. They all have expensive cars, clothes, shoes, purebred dogs, cats, and horses, and houses big enough to hold lavish parties with all of their (often backstabbing) friends.*

I do not envy them. But they are very entertaining when one is stuck in bed and under the influence of pain meds.

Dear Ma,

Summer is coming. I think you would be gratified to know I can now wear a bikini if I choose! Not that I have never in the past worn one, but as a young girl, when I came home from a shopping trip with my friend Babs, and showed you my new baby blue and white striped two-piece, which had ties on the sides that, if pulled tight and then twisted into bows, would magically transform the waist-high bottoms into bikini bottoms, you immediately disapproved. Not because of any moral issue or a desire to turn me into a conservative teenager, but because of my belly button. It was an outie. It was, you advised me, not to be seen in public.

I tied the ties anyway and will say I don't recall anyone ever growing nauseous over my physical imperfection. But man, it bothered you tremendously.

Let me say right now, on the record, not many things I did bothered you. But this was a battle you never gave up. Well, I wish you were here to see me now!

A few weeks ago on a Tuesday, I drove up to the Bay Area to see you and have lunch together. You were so restless and agitated and didn't want to sit and eat the split pea soup and lasagna. We walked up and down the hallway and nodded hello to your fellow residents in the assisted living facility, you with your walker and me with my hand at the small of your back. Your caregivers smiled as we walked back and forth, back and forth. When you grew tired, we returned to your room where you stretched out on your bed and I pulled up a chair to sit next to you. I held your hand and you looked deep into my eyes. I could see you struggling to sort out your thoughts. There was a look of panic in your blue eyes. You were trying so hard to make sense of things. But all was a jumble and I could see the fear and frustration on your face. After what seemed like a minute, you wanted up again.

We walked the halls and said hello to all we passed once more. Some responded; others simply stared.

We practiced reading the room numbers as a way to remind you of your own room number. And when we returned to your small apartment, you stood and read your name and number out loud and smiled at your success.

I asked you if you were hungry. If you would like me to go and get your abandoned lunch and bring it to you.

"Just the cake," you replied, which I thought showed great brilliance. It was your favorite vanilla cake with strawberries and whipped cream.

I hurried back to the dining area and got not one piece, but two. When I showed you, you smiled. I wanted you to enjoy them both, but you wouldn't have it.

So we had cake together.

I thought of all the angel food cakes you had made over the years. Angel food cake with whipped cream. Not just plain whipped cream; you would add powdered Nesquik to the cream while you whipped it giving it a faint taste of chocolate. Each bite melted in your mouth. Light and airy, it was a perfect sweet treat.

This strawberry cream cake was almost as good. Or maybe it was just that I was sharing it with you.

When it was time for me to leave, you wanted to walk me to the elevator. Once there, you noticed one of your favorite caregivers, Mario, and began to follow him down the hall back towards your room.

The elevator dinged and you turned around and looked at me with panic. "I've got her," said Mario, smiling. And he told me to go.

I stood and watched you, your hair as white as egret feathers. Your shoulders bent, your hands gripping your walker. Your turquoise cotton pants bagging in the seat. You had lost so much weight in the past few weeks. You looked so frail. So small.

It gave me comfort to know that Mario would take care of you. It also gave me some kind of comfort to know that, within moments of my leaving, you would not even remember I had been there. You would not miss me because you had no memory of my visit.

I had no idea that I would never see you again. That this was our last moment together. You walking with Mario, me waiting for the elevator.

Your sagging summer pants.

It was a long, slow drive home. My friend Leonard Cohen kept me company. I sang along with him as I drove up and over the Santa Cruz Mountains.

The next morning, my gut busted. Surgery was performed late that night. The next five days, I was in the hospital and thought about how odd it was that you had no idea where I was. I knew there was no point in having someone tell you. You would have worried and gotten confused and then forgotten all about it. So what was the point? But still, strange to be so unwell and not be able to share the news with you. To be unable to call my mother.

The healing was slow. My goal was to be well enough to drive back over the mountain so I could see you. I wanted to show you the results of the surgery. My outie belly button is gone! I now, as near as I can tell, have only a small indentation where it once used to be! I couldn't wait to share the news!

After five days, I finally got to go home, and my dear friend, Becky visited every day. She brought me smoothies she made at home. She kept close watch on me, like a good sister/friend.

I was curled up in my own bed when my phone rang. It was Cheryl's husband, Howie. He was calling to tell me you had died in your sleep. I had no idea how to deal with the news. I wanted to rush to you once more to hold your hand. To brush your hair. To kiss your cheek. To see you.

It was a physical impossibility. I wasn't even able to attend your funeral. But I wrote something, and

Michael, dear, wonderful Michael, attended and read the eulogy.

I did not mention my belly button.

That is something just between the two of us.

The bandages came off today. Where there had always been a round, fat little button there is nothing but a tiny tuck. There is still some bruising and swelling, but in time that will fade. My button, it seems, is gone.

Ma, you would be so happy!

I wish there was a way to let you know.

To be honest, even with my new and improved abdomen I doubt I will spring for a new bikini. The rest of my body, as reliable as it is, and as much as I appreciate having it, it is far from toned. It is 68 years old and there is a bit of obvious wear and tear. But still, it is amazing to think that what drove you nuts when I was a teenager is now gone!

This morning in the shower, I tenderly washed the area where, for nine months, you and I were attached. All signs of that physical bond are gone. As gone as you are now.

Standing in the warm, gentle spray, I kept thinking of you and how, when I was a newborn, you gently washed my round little belly with the doorbell button and loved me no matter what.

For that and absolutely everything else, thank you.

Love forever,
Claudia

Dear Cheryl,

Where to begin. In a few months we will be marking the fifth anniversary of Carol's leaving us. How can that be?

Remember the afternoon I drove up to the Bay Area to meet with you and your therapist? You had called and asked if I would and I wanted so badly to understand what had happened and how it might be fixed that I said yes, of course.

Michael wasn't sure if I should go. He reminded me that in the many months since Carol had died, not once had you offered an apology or actual explanation for that night, or any of the hurtful events which followed.

"But this time maybe she will," I told him. "Maybe she will."

I was nervous as I made my way over the Santa Cruz Mountains and through the traffic towards your therapist's office. All the way there I kept trying to imagine what to expect.

It was a warm day and the sun so bright, the glare bouncing off cars as I walked through the parking lot towards the building, blinding me. Once inside, I searched the directory for the name of your therapist and made my way to her office.

I don't remember if you were there when I arrived or joined me after a few minutes. I just recall how awkward it felt to be alone with you in the small waiting room making even smaller talk. There wasn't an elephant in the room; there was an entire zoo. I don't know what was going through your mind as we waited, but I felt as if we couldn't talk about why we were there until we had a professional to help guide us. I was very self-conscious about coming across as overly emotional. Overly dramatic.

Your therapist was late. We waited for almost a half an hour and, when she entered the waiting room, she seemed surprised, then apologetic at her tardiness.

She had a bandage covering the tip of her nose, which distracted me, I will admit.

She went into her office and stated she would come out to get us in just a few minutes, which she did.

She seemed nice enough. I don't know how long you had been seeing her, but she seemed familiar with our problem.

"Can you tell me how you remember what happened that night in Carol's bedroom?" she asked me.

So, I recounted the experience from my perspective. She looked at you and asked if that was accurate.

It was, you told her. And then you were quiet.

The quieter you became, the more frustrated I became. And once again, when I asked why you had allowed Carol's wife to say such terrible things, you shrugged your shoulders, pursed your lips and remained silent.

Then you stated once more that I am different.

The therapist agreed that I was obviously more emotional, pointing out that, while your hands remained in your lap still, mine were flapping around like a bird trying to take flight.

Then, fuck me if I didn't begin to cry. Again.

I looked at you and said how much it hurt to have been cut out. How much it hurt to have had my phone calls refused. To have been told that my help, so needed at the time, was now seen as an irritant rather than a blessing.

I said how sad it made me that you had had a gathering of people to scatter Carol's ashes and I was not included. And that another ash-scattering event had taken place with friends in Italy.

Your therapist asked if this were true and you nodded.

At one point, you claimed that Carol's wife and I had a fight.

That, I had to correct. There was no fight. That would be like calling Pearl Harbor a fight. No. Bombs were dropped with no warning. It was an attack, pure and simple.

Cheryl, my dear little sister, part of me was incredibly impressed. You were always the "softest" of the twins. But over time, you seem to have been able to build a spine of steel.

You were the twin who bowed to Carol's wishes growing up. She called the shots and you went along.

You were the willow, she the oak.

How many mornings when we were small did Carol choose which dress to wear to school and force you to wear the same? And after school, it was Carol who would decide if you were going to go out and play baseball or ride skateboards.

She was two minutes older than you and she used that to an advantage.

But now, there we were in your therapist's office, and you were not going to give an inch. You are tougher than I ever imagined.

You looked at me and said, "Are you asking me to choose?" I assumed you meant choose between me and Carol's wife.

I was struck by the question, as it was so obvious that you already had. All those months earlier in Carol's bedroom, you clearly chose.

But Cheryl, may I say, I have never stopped loving you. Sitting in that hot, stuffy office with sweat running down my back and tears running down my face, all of the pain was because I do love you. And I loved Carol.

Feeling as if there was no longer a point to the meeting, I stood up and said I was going home. We had used up most of the hour anyway and I knew that no progress had been made.

How many times could I sit and listen to you say again and again that I just am not like you or Carol or Carol's wife and that that is the problem?

I never claimed to be the same. I just never knew that in your mind and heart, different was wrong.

Oh, Cheryl, I want you to be happy. I firmly believe that losing Carol was the most difficult thing to ever happen to you. I had hoped that I might be a comfort to you after she was gone. That our bond as sisters would gain in strength.

Perhaps I would be able to sleep at night if you had been able to articulate what you really needed. Perhaps becoming the soulmate of Carol's wife has made you feel closer to Carol?

Perhaps if you had explained that to me, rather than just silently shutting me out, I could move on.

There have been times over the past few months that we have spoken on the phone. Conversations about our mother. Or dealing with Carol's estate. Your voice always sounds cheery and light.

I am always taken aback by that. I don't know if it means you are happy with how things have turned out, or that you are pretending none of it happened. But it is true when you say we are different because I can't do that. Because I loved you and Carol so much, so deeply, that something broke in me. It has to be mended before it can even begin to heal.

Last month, Michael took me to Hawaii again. I had no great expectations about the trip. I recalled the vacation we took soon after Carol died and how difficult it was for me. How I believed I was supposed to be thrilled to be with my husband in the lush tropical environment and yet everything just felt flat. I was afraid things would be the same this time as well. I even told him about my apprehension. I was terrified of disappointing him as well as myself. He understood. He is so very patient.

We checked into the resort on Hawaii's Kona Coast where we would be for five days. We were part of a large group of sales people from the Western United States who had sold an abundance of farming equipment and were given the trip as a reward. Michael, who still works at the tractor dealership, was one of the winners.

Oh, Cheryl. It was beautiful. There was a rocky beach where turtles sunned themselves, and a small lagoon for swimming and snorkeling. We began each day with breakfast in bed and then would head to the lagoon for the afternoon. I began to actually relax in a way that I haven't for longer than I care to think.

Three days in, I thought, yes. This is good. I am doing it. I am enjoying myself! I watched paddle boarders as they balanced on their boards and skimmed across the turquoise water and felt a bond with them. I, too, was finding my balance and skimming across the surface of my life. I felt the warm breeze. Felt my shoulders relax.

On our next to last day, Michael and I decided to rent a car and drive up the coast to the northern most tip of the island. I had woken up that morning feeling emotionally off for the first time since we had arrived. I decided I would keep quiet and try to just push through. The previous days had been so good. Surely, I could right my emotions. Find my balance once again.

We drove along the coast listening to pop music on the radio, and Michael, distracted by the extravagant views, didn't seem to notice my silence.

The further we drove, the more tense I became. I have recognized over the years that when I slip into this dark place it isn't just emotional, it becomes physical. My stomach knots, my eyes fill, I spend an inordinate amount of time biting the inside of my cheek to try to keep my feelings trapped.

By the time we reached the Pololu Valley Lookout, I was about as shut down as one could be.

It is a spectacular spot. High on a bluff overlooking a deep canyon. The hike to the bottom is steep. So steep that walking sticks are needed to go up and down. We parked the car and Michael walked to the edge and gazed out at the view. I hung back. I realized with great clarity that I did not want to place myself anywhere near the precipice.

I was not afraid I would fall. I was afraid I might jump.

Back in the car, Michael looked at me, really looked, and saw what was happening. And the relief in his knowing was so great I began to cry.

I am just so tired, I told him. So exhausted from carrying this with me everywhere I go.

And as soon as I said it, I realized what I had to do. I had to set it down. I have to stop carrying you and that night and all that has happened since around with me. It is simply too heavy. The burden too much.

I am letting you go. I am no longer searching for answers.

Michael told me not long ago that on the morning we drove up to Carol's house so that I could see her one last time, he, while waiting with you downstairs, asked you why. Why you had chosen to do what you did. Why then of all times, with Carol dying and all of us devastated by that fact, why you decided it was the time to say the things you said.

Why?

He told me you just stared at the floor and remained silent. While I was upstairs with Carol and her wife trying to soothe our sister in her last hours.

Why.

Oh, Cheryl, those three small letters are so heavy to carry. I am setting them down. I am done asking the question.

As I write this, you and Carol's wife are on a cruise. From what I hear, this has become a regular occurrence. I assume you enjoy the view from the deck, the shows in the evening, the food and drinks and festivities. I pray you do. I mean that sincerely.

Someday, when your grandchildren get older, I hope you will tell them that you once had two sisters. One, your twin, your other half, whom you loved deeply and fully, and the other, older by two and a half years, who, even though quite different, you loved as well.

This is what I plan on telling my Darling Boy.

Once upon a time, there were three little Nielsen girls. The twins, joined in more ways than one could imagine, and the older one, the singular one, who made her way through life on her own. Making mistakes here and there. Slightly envious of the twins who were a team.

What might it have been like to have a sister so close. One who could read my mind and I hers. To have been born with a lifetime companion.

I flailed around latching on to men who were not a good match, but were available for companionship. I was looking for my "other." I finally found it in Michael.

You were born with yours.

Here is where I feel the deepest sadness for you, Cheryl. Because to have never been singular, and then after so long to find yourself in that unexpected, terrible, nightmarish position, I can understand why you would need to cling to someone.

I had just hoped it would be me.

I love you, I love you, I love you,
Claude

P.S. We did do something together. We made sure Ma never knew what happened between us. Excellent team work.

Dear Reader,

Hello? Are you still with me? If so, many thanks for indulging me. I realize it was asking a lot. I mean, who even writes letters anymore? Who is interested in reading them? If you raised your hand, I am grateful.

When was the last time you picked up a pen and paper and started a conversation with an old friend, family member, or even a stranger? Think about giving it a go. It can be deeply satisfying.

Drop me a line anytime!

Respectfully,
Claudia

Dear Michael,

You mentioned the other day that I seem better. More relaxed. Sometimes, happy. You are right.

I am.

I love you so much.

Yours,
Claudia

Author's Note

There are those in my life I cannot thank enough for supporting me when I began this project. My "sister-friends" who encouraged me throughout, especially Kathy Chetkovich, Jonathan Franzen's "Californian", who, on every beach walk we took, asked about the letters. It was she who read them one by one as I produced them and told me to keep going. There were more beach walks than I can count, and, with every sandy step, she filled my heart with encouraging words.

I wish I could thank my doctor, Dr. A., who with his calm voice and deep understanding of grief helped me just keep going. Oh, how I do miss him.

I am grateful to my lovely, sassy agent, Charlotte Gusay who over French pastries in a small cafe in Beverly Hills said, "Let's do this!"

To my publisher, Steven Radecki, and the folks at Paper Angel Press for seeing something in this collection that they thought others may want to read. Fingers crossed you are all correct!

Lastly, to my Darling Boy who brought so much light to my life I was almost blinded. Love is such a small word to describe what I feel for you. All the stars in the heavens, all the fish in the sea don't add up to the joy you have given me.

About the Author

Claudia Sternbach is the author of two previous memoirs, *Now Breathe, a very personal journey through breast cancer* (Whiteaker Press) and *Reading Lips, a memoir of kisses* (Unbridled Books).

Claudia was a newspaper columnist for many years and has been published often in *The San Francisco Chronicle*, *The San Francisco Examiner*, and *The Chicago Tribune*. She has also been published in several anthologies and is the former editor-in-chief of the literary journal, *Memoir*.

When she isn't writing, Claudia paints. When she isn't writing or painting, she can be found on her daily walk on the beach. And at the end of the day she enjoys a cocktail on her back yard swing while watching the squirrels trapeze branch to branch in the redwoods. Claudia lives on the coast of Northern California with her husband, Michael.

CPSIA information can be obtained
at www.ICGtesting.com
Printed in the USA
BVHW040204031221
623152BV00011B/297/J